100 DISASTERS

THAT SHAPED WORLD HISTORY

JOANNE MATTERN

sourcebooks
eXplore

Copyright © 2023 by Sourcebooks
Text by Joanne Mattern
Cover design by Will Riley
Internal illustrations by Westchester Publishing Services
Cover and internal design © 2023 by Sourcebooks

Sourcebooks and the colophon are registered trademarks of Sourcebooks.

Published by Sourcebooks eXplore, an imprint of Sourcebooks Kids
P.O. Box 4410, Naperville, Illinois 60567-4410
(630) 961-3900
sourcebookskids.com

Cataloging-in-Publication Data is on file with the Library of Congress.

Source of Production: Versa Press, East Peoria, Illinois, USA
Date of Production: July 2023
Trade Paperback ISBN: 9781728290089 Run Number: 5032106
Hardcover ISBN: 9781728290096 Run Number: 5032110

Printed and bound in the United States of America.
VP 10 9 8 7 6 5 4 3 2 1

CONTENTS

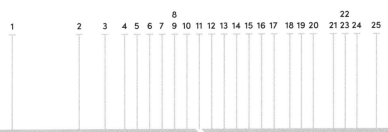

Timeline of Disasters

79 CE   1930

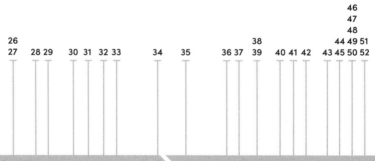

Timeline of Disasters

1930   1980

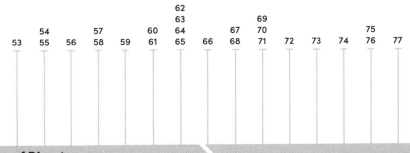

Timeline of Disasters

1980   1994

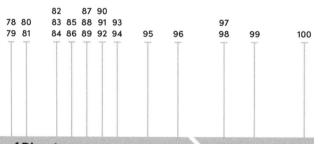

Timeline of Disasters

1995

2020

INTRODUCTION

Terrible storms, devastating earthquakes, powerful explosions...disasters come in many different forms. Some—tornadoes, hurricanes, floods, droughts—are caused by bad weather. Some, such as volcano eruptions and earthquakes, are caused by natural changes in the earth. Still more have human causes—train wrecks, plane crashes, burning buildings, oil spills, and nuclear dangers.

Some disasters are noteworthy because of the number of people who perished because of them. Some of these totals are hard to comprehend, such as the estimated 500,000 killed by the Bhola cyclone in 1970. Other disasters may not claim many lives, but they level cities or destroy large portions of the environment, like the Great Fire of London in 1666 and the oil spill caused by the Exxon *Valdez*. Some disasters, such as pandemics of deadly diseases, are truly worldwide in scope.

Whatever form they take, disasters have fascinated people for thousands of years. From ancient civilizations to today, our histories record a variety of disasters. The ancient Greeks described how the Colossus of Rhodes, one of the Seven Wonders of the Ancient World, was destroyed by an earthquake around 225 B.C. Today's new sources frequently report on details of tragedies and destruction.

Why are people so fascinated by horrific accounts of death and destruction? Often, we are drawn to the personal stories involved. The tragic loss of life on the *Titanic*, for example, has been made into several popular movies and countless books. Other times we are simply awed by the destructive power of nature, demonstrated in a hurricane or tornado, or baffled by the error in human judgement displayed in so many mechanical failures or crashes.

It is also humbling to realize how suddenly a disaster can strike and change lives forever. Earthquakes destroy cities in a matter of seconds, and a plane can fall out of the sky with no warning. Why do these things happen? How can we cope with such stunning events? Reading about disasters gives us a chance to ponder these questions and, possibly, come up with answers that make sense to us, and solutions to ensure fewer disasters in the future.

Disasters also show us how one event can change history. Ireland's potato famine during the 1840s sent a wave of immigrants to America to start a new life, changing the face of the United States forever. Tragic fires such as the Cocoanut Grove or the MGM Grand changed laws and building requirements, preventing future loss of life. Terrorist attacks have created heightened security protocols and changed the way people go about their daily lives.

This book features 100 disasters, and covers almost 2,000 years, from the volcanic eruption that buried the Roman town of Pompeii in 79 A.D. to more recent events like the Fukushima Daiichi nuclear disaster in 2011. Included are many different kinds of disasters—earthquakes, tornadoes, explosions, mining accidents, and even a molasses flood. These disasters took place all over the world, from remote villages to huge cities, proving that events can go out of control anytime and anyplace.

Along with well-known disasters, such as the sinking of the *Titanic*, the 1906 San Francisco earthquake, and the terrorist attacks of September 11, 2001, this book includes less publicized events too. However, it is by no means meant to be a comprehensive list of disasters. Some events, though devastating in scope, were unable to be included because of a lack of information.

For example, in the last century, China has had many floods and earthquakes with death tolls in the hundreds of thousands, but the Chinese government released very few details of these calamities. Similarly, it is often difficult to find information about events that happened hundreds of years ago, since records from ancient times are often incomplete or lost entirely. This book should serve as an introduction to the many different disasters that have struck our world and changed lives throughout history.

Time stopped in the Italian cities of **Pompeii** and **Herculaneum** on August 24, 79 CE. That morning, a volcanic eruption buried the two towns, hiding them from the world for centuries.

Pompeii was a large town in the kingdom of **Rome** (now southern Italy). Herculaneum was a small town about ten miles northwest of Pompeii. Both towns lay in the shadow of **Mount Vesuvius**, an active volcano that towered 4,190 feet above the **Bay of Naples**.

August 24 was a normal summer day in both towns. Shops opened, and people went about their daily chores. Families gathered together to share meals. In Herculaneum, a festival was being held to honor Rome's first emperor.

Suddenly, there was a deafening crack. The earth shook. Then the whole top of Mount Vesuvius broke open, releasing a flood of red-hot lava. Along with the lava came huge rocks, waves of mud, and a thick cloud of smoke and dust.

Thousands of residents fled in terror, trying to escape the choking clouds and the hot chunks of burning lava raining down on them. A Roman writer named **Pliny the Younger** later wrote that the terrible darkness was "not a moonless night, but the darkness of a sealed room."

By the time the wave of mud, lava, and dust ended, Pompeii and Herculaneum were nowhere to be seen. The entire area was covered by a thick layer of ash and mud. Streets, buildings, homes... Everything had disappeared. In Herculaneum, the lava and mud were so thick that they hardened into an 80-foot-deep layer of solid rock.

Historians think that about two thousand people were killed in Pompeii alone. Some were buried in the mud. Others died when buildings collapsed. Many more suffocated from breathing in dust, ash, and smoke.

The sites of Pompeii and Herculaneum were abandoned, and in time, the Romans forgot all about these ancient cities. Many centuries later, people digging in the soil occasionally found pieces of marble or statues in the area around Mount Vesuvius. Realizing that there were cities under the ground, scientists and other people tried to excavate whatever they could. On December 11, 1738, men working for the Spanish king **Charles III** discovered the Theater of Herculaneum. Pompeii was discovered twenty-five years later, on August 16, 1763.

Amazing artifacts emerged from Pompeii and Herculaneum, including lamps, pottery, statues, jewelry, and paintings. Then buildings and streets were uncovered. Workers also found skeletons of both people and animals preserved in the mud.

Unfortunately, the excavations caused a great deal of damage to the sites. Many valuable artifacts were destroyed because workers were careless or did not know how to preserve the objects they found. Other items were stolen or damaged by bad weather. As excavation techniques improved, more buildings and artifacts were able to be preserved.

Today, Pompeii and Herculaneum are tourist sites and living museums. Artifacts from these lost towns have been exhibited around the world, giving modern people a chance to step into the past and catch a glimpse of everyday life almost two thousand years ago.

The **Bubonic Plague** is one of the deadliest diseases ever known. In just four years during the Middle Ages, this disease killed a third of Europe's population, and changed society forever.

The first symptom of the bubonic plague was swollen, dark lymph nodes called "**buboes**." A bubo could become as large as an orange and would get very painful. The patient also suffered from a high fever, headaches, and weakness. Some patients coughed up blood. Death usually followed in a few days as there was no treatment for this terrible disease.

A plague doctor wearing a mask meant to prevent the wearer from catching the disease

The plague arrived in Europe in October 1347, when twelve merchant ships from **Caffa** in the Middle East arrived in **Messina**, Italy. Most of the sailors and passengers were dead or dying. City officials worried that whatever disease had killed the sailors would spread through Messina, so they said that no person or cargo could leave the ships. However, no one paid any attention to the **rats** running on and off. These rats were infected with the plague, too, and they soon spread the disease to Messina's citizens. Within two months, half the people in the city were dead.

Other Italian port cities were also struck by the plague. Then, the disease spread to **Germany**, **France**, **England**, **Norway**, and **Russia**. It traveled via rats, trade ships, and people fleeing cities where the disease had already struck.

So many people fell ill with the plague that normal life was impossible. People were afraid to go to work or even leave their homes. Homes and stores were abandoned. Soldiers were too sick to defend citizens, and officials could not govern cities. The only thing people could do was pray that they wouldn't get sick. Many thought that it was the end of the world.

Usually, the plague struck cities or towns for two or three months at a time. Then, the disease ran its course and stopped. By 1351, the plague was over. Twenty-five million people had died.

Before the plague, peasants were bound to one lord and were forced to work for poor wages in subpar living conditions. But the plague killed so many and there were only a few peasants left alive to work. This shortage of workers allowed people to demand better wages and conditions. If one employer refused their demands, it was not hard to find a job with someone else.

A smaller population also meant more resources for those who were still alive. More food and better shelter were available, and people had more money to spend. Goods were scarce, which meant that craftspeople could charge more money for them. In time, these developments led to better living conditions and helped create a financially stable middle class.

There would be other outbreaks of the plague over the next few centuries. Even today, the bubonic plague is still a threat in parts of the world, although we now have antibiotics to fight it. Alas, no outbreak to date has been as devastating as the **Black Death** and its sweep across Europe in the 1300s.

Accidental fires were nothing new in London during the 1600s. Open fires were used for cooking and heating, and most buildings were made of wood or plaster, with straw laid on the floors. These highly flammable conditions led to one of the most devastating fires in history.

The night of Sunday, September 2, 1666, smoldering embers from a baker's oven ignited a stack of firewood. By morning, the whole building was on fire. A strong wind spread the flames through the neighborhood. In just a few hours, three hundred buildings were destroyed.

There were no public fire departments in 1666. Instead, citizens put out fires by pouring buckets of water on them. They also used iron hooks and ropes to pull down buildings in the fire's path to create a firebreak. These methods were no match for the Great Fire.

Panicked residents fled the disaster, packing boats along the **Thames River** and filling the streets leading away from the blaze. To protect money and valuables, many people buried them or hid them in the sewers. Police tried to stop thieves from looting abandoned homes and businesses.

On Tuesday, the fire spread north and west, eventually destroying **Old St. Paul's Cathedral**. A witness named John Evelyn wrote in his diary: "The stones of Paul's flew like granados [grenades], the melting lead running down the streets in a stream and the very pavements glowing with fiery redness."

Soldiers created a large firebreak by exploding stores of gunpowder to save the **Tower of London** and the eastern part of the city. Then, on Wednesday morning, the wind

died down and the fire lost its intensity. By Thursday night, the fire was finally out.

The **Great Fire of London** destroyed more than thirteen thousand houses, eighty-seven churches, and many public buildings. Although only five people died, up to two hundred thousand lost their homes and everything they owned.

Londoners quickly set about rebuilding their city, planning a whole new look. Streets were widened and building height restrictions were codified. These changes led to more open avenues and less crowded conditions. Regulations also stated that new buildings had to be constructed of brick or stone instead of wood to cut down on the danger of fire.

The greatest building to rise from London's ashes was the new **St. Paul's Cathedral**, designed by the renowned architect **Christopher Wren**. This magnificent new church was the largest in Europe and remains one of the city's most important landmarks today. Wren designed fifty other churches following the Great Fire.

The Great Fire cost the City of London about ten million pounds, which was an astronomical amount of money in 1666. The high cost and tremendous damage led to the formation of private fire insurance societies. People bought insurance for their property from fire companies and were given an identifying plaque to display on the front of the building. If the building caught fire, the company's private fire department came to the rescue. This arrangement lasted for two hundred years, until the city took over fire protection in 1866.

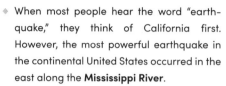

When most people hear the word "earthquake," they think of California first. However, the most powerful earthquake in the continental United States occurred in the east along the **Mississippi River**.

Between December 1811 and February 1812, the area around **New Madrid, Missouri**, was rocked by three powerful earthquakes. The first struck at about two o'clock in the morning of December 16. Eyewitnesses reported hearing a thunderous, vibrating noise. Trees cracked and fell, and the Mississippi River became so violent that it actually flowed backward for a few minutes. Terrified citizens and animals ran out of their houses and barns, not knowing what was happening or when it would end.

The earthquake caused damage all the way to **Charleston, South Carolina**, and **Washington, DC.** The vibrations even rang church bells in **Boston, Massachusetts**, which was over 1,000 miles away!

Small aftershocks after the December 16 quake were followed by another strong shake on January 23, 1812. For days after the January event, the earth moved due to aftershocks, described by one woman, **Eliza Bryan**, as "visibly waving as a gentle sea." Then, on February 4, another even more powerful earthquake struck the New Madrid area.

Eliza Bryan recalled: "The Mississippi seemed to recede from its banks, and its waters gathering up like a mountain... It then rising fifteen to twenty feet perpendicularly, and expanding, as it were, at the same moment, the banks were overflowed with the retrograde current, rapid as a torrent... The river falling immediately, as rapid as it had risen, receded in its banks again with such violence, that it took with it whole grove of young cottonwood trees." The quake filled the river with dozens of damaged or destroyed boats, and the ground was also violently affected. After the quake, the site of New Madrid was fifteen feet lower than its previous location, and most of the land ended up under the Mississippi River. Many ponds and lakes in the area had dried up, while others were lifted twenty feet higher. The quake also created new channels for the Mississippi River. Many residents were so frightened that they moved away from the area, never to return.

Scientists later figured out that the New Madrid earthquakes measured between 8.4 and 8.7 on the Richter scale—more powerful than any other earthquake in the United States. Fortunately, because the area was so sparsely populated, there were only six confirmed fatalities. However, a major fault line runs through the area, so scientists do worry that major quakes could strike there again. Since the area is now home to millions of people and many major cities, another quake like the ones of 1811–1812 would cause billions of dollars in damage and kill thousands of people.

Some disasters are sudden. Earthquakes, storms, or explosions can cause tremendous loss of life in just a few minutes. But other disasters unfold more slowly over time, quietly killing thousands, or even millions of people. The **Irish potato famine** of the 1840s was just such a disaster.

During the 1800s, Ireland was under British control, and peasant farmers worked on property owned by British landlords. Although farmers grew oats, wheat, and barley, and raised cattle, sheep, and pigs, almost all the food supplies were sent to Great Britain. That left the potato as the only source of sustenance for the farmers. Large numbers of potatoes could be grown in small plots of land, and just one acre of potatoes could feed an entire family of six. People ate several pounds of potatoes every day for their whole lives.

Disaster struck in the fall of 1845, however, when a mysterious fungus, or **blight**, suddenly struck the crops. Almost overnight, the potatoes turned into a slimy, horrible-smelling, black mush. Potatoes that still looked healthy were quickly dug out of the ground, but they had already been contaminated with the fungus and started to rot. Almost half of the potato crop yield in 1845 was lost. For the next few years, there would be almost no potato crop at all.

Without potatoes to eat, Irish farming families began to starve. Even though there was not enough food for the Irish, they were still expected to ship produce to their landlords in Great Britain. Meanwhile, the Irish were forced to eat grass in a desperate attempt to stay alive.

Starving farmers were unable to work or grow enough food to pay the rent on the farmland, and thousands were evicted from their homes. They dug holes in the earth and covered them with straw or turf for shelter.

People weakened by starvation were easy prey for disease. Epidemics of cholera, typhoid, and dysentery raced through communities, killing thousands. In one community, 169 people died in three weeks. It was not unusual for officials to enter a house and find entire families dead inside.

The potato blight continued for ten years, although some years were worse than others. By 1855, the land was free of the fungus and could produce potatoes again. But the damage had already been done. A million Irish peasants had died of starvation or disease. More than 1.5 million others left Ireland forever, emigrating to Great Britain, the United States, and Canada. Many British landlords went bankrupt, or were attacked and even killed by angry mobs as retribution for starving the Irish people.

The potato famine became one of the most important events in history. It was the greatest disaster ever to strike Ireland, and it changed the country forever. Indeed, the famine changed American history as well because it created one of the largest immigrant communities in the United States that would become a major force in American life and culture.

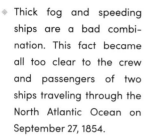

Thick fog and speeding ships are a bad combination. This fact became all too clear to the crew and passengers of two ships traveling through the North Atlantic Ocean on September 27, 1854.

The **SS Arctic** was a wooden paddle wheeler, and one of the fastest passenger ships on the ocean. It was owned by the **Collins Line**, an American company, and ran regularly between England and the United States. On September 27, the ship was on its way home to New York.

About sixty miles from the coast of Newfoundland, the *Arctic* ran into a bank of heavy fog. Most captains would have slowed the ship because of the poor visibility. But **Captain James C. Luce** ordered the *Arctic* to keep going at full speed.

Suddenly, another ship loomed out of the fog. It was the French steamship **SS Vesta**. The *Vesta* rammed into the side of the *Arctic*, ripping three holes in the wooden ship. The *Vesta* was also damaged and began to sink.

Although the *Arctic* was taking on water, Luce didn't think his own ship was too badly damaged. He decided to continue on to Newfoundland as fast as he could. This turned out to be a very bad idea.

The faster the *Arctic* traveled, the more water rushed into the ship. Waves flooded the boilers and engines, cutting off the ship's power. The ship was still about twenty miles from land when it began to sink.

Captain Luce called his 368 passengers and crew members on deck and told them to get off the ship. When the crew realized that there were not enough lifeboats for everyone, they began to panic. Some crew members rushed the lifeboats, knocking women and children out of their way. When an officer drew his gun to fire a warning blast in the air, a crew member hit him over the head with a shovel, killing him.

Only two boats carrying thirty-one crew members and fourteen passengers made it to Newfoundland. Other victims survived by clinging to pieces of wood and other debris. They were finally picked up by another ship two days later.

The *Vesta*, meanwhile, fared much better. Her captain ordered all cargo thrown into the sea to lighten the ship. This tactic worked, and the *Vesta* was able to steam slowly into port with no loss of life.

Only about sixty-eight people survived the disaster. One of them was Captain Luce. The collision haunted him until the end of his life. His young son was killed in the accident along with the wife and two children of Edward Collins, owner of the Collins Line. Collins never forgave Luce and publicly called him a murderer.

The *Arctic–Vesta* collision was the beginning of the end for the Collins Line. After another Collins ship, the **SS Pacific,** vanished during a transatlantic crossing in 1856, people were afraid to sail with the company. The Collins Line went out of business in the early 1860s. Meanwhile, the wreck from the *Arctic* remains at the bottom of the ocean.

Some disasters go almost unnoticed, even though they claim many lives. Such was the case of the **Sultana** steamboat explosion, a virtually unknown event that is still considered America's worst naval disaster.

The **American Civil War** had ended just a few weeks before the *Sultana*'s fatal voyage in late April of 1865. Thousands of Union soldiers were being released from southern prison camps, and many gathered in Vicksburg, Mississippi, to board Mississippi River steamboats and make their way home.

The *Sultana* left New Orleans on April 21 and arrived in Vicksburg on April 24, ready to take on the Union soldiers. However, an engineer discovered that one of the ship's boilers was leaking, and the trip had to be delayed for thirty-three hours while it was repaired. Meanwhile, the former prisoners of war (POWs) swarmed onto the ship. Although the *Sultana* was only allowed to carry 376 people, about seventeen hundred to twenty-two hundred passengers crammed into the steamer.

After the *Sultana*'s boiler was repaired, it left Vicksburg and headed up the river to Memphis, landing on the morning of April 26. Around midnight, the ship set off again. By three o'clock in the morning on April 27, the overcrowded ship was a few miles above Memphis.

Suddenly, the repaired boiler exploded with a tremendous crash that could be heard back in Memphis. Chunks of wood, machinery, furniture, and other pieces of the ship flew into the water. The passengers, many of whom had been asleep, were blown overboard. Most were so weakened by their time in the prison camps that they could not fight the river's strong current and drowned.

The ship became a ball of fire as burning coal from the boilers blew onto the deck. The smokestacks fell, crushing many men beneath them. Desperate passengers leaped into the water. One survivor recalled, "I would see men jumping from all parts of the boat into the water until it seemed black with men, their heads bobbing up and down like corks, and then disappearing beneath the turbulent waters, never to appear again."

The burning *Sultana* floated downstream, finally crashing into a small island and sinking. When the sun rose a few hours later, rescuers found survivors and bodies for miles along both sides of the river. For days afterward, a barge ventured out each morning to collect the dead and bring their bodies back to Memphis. Estimates of the death toll ranged from fifteen hundred to nineteen hundred.

The cause of the boiler explosion was never determined. The Union army was criticized for overcrowding the boat when other ships had been available to take returning soldiers north.

Despite the huge loss of life, the *Sultana* disaster soon disappeared from newspapers and public attention. Americans were soon more concerned with the death of **President Abraham Lincoln**, who was assassinated on April 14, and the end of the Civil War. Today, the *Sultana* disaster remains one of the deadliest—and least known—maritime accidents.

◆ Can a cow cause a big conflagration? Many people believe one cow started a huge fire that devastated the city of **Chicago** in 1871. However, the truth is not always what it seems.

The summer and fall of 1871 had been hot and dry in the Midwestern United States. There had been many fires in Chicago that summer, as sparks set fire to dry leaves, hay, and wood shavings and kindling used to start cooking fires. Most of the city's buildings were made of

wood with tar-covered roofs, which made them highly flammable. Even the roads and sidewalks were made of wood to keep them from sinking in the muddy, swampy ground.

At nine o'clock on Sunday evening, October 8, a watchman spotted smoke and flames. A fire had started in a barn owned by **Patrick and Catherine O'Leary**, who ran a dairy business. The barn was filled with hay, coal, and wood, which fed the fire. By the time firefighters arrived, the blaze was already out of control. Flames rose five hundred feet into the air, and the winds blew burning chunks of wood throughout the city, starting new fires wherever the embers landed. The blaze even leaped across the Chicago River, driven on by the powerful wind. Residents fled, and many found shelter along Lake Michigan's beaches. As the fire drew closer, the evacuees waded into the freezing water to stay safe.

The *Chicago Post* described the fire roaring through the city: "The earth and sky were fire and flames; the atmosphere was smoke... Great sheets of flames literally flapped in the air like sails on shipboard..."

Although firefighters came from as far away as Pittsburgh and Cincinnati to help, Chicago burned for twenty-seven hours until a rainstorm late Monday night put out the worst of the flames. The fire had destroyed 17,500 buildings and left 100,000 people homeless. About three hundred people were killed, but many bodies were never recovered.

Everyone wanted to know how the fire had started. A rumor said that Mrs. O'Leary had been using a kerosene lamp for light while she was milking a cow. The rumor has it that the cow kicked over the lamp, starting the fire. Even though the O'Leary family was in bed when the fire started and not milking cows, this story spread throughout the country and even became a popular song. In fact, no one is sure what started the Chicago fire. It may have been a cigarette carelessly dropped near the barn or a case of spontaneous combustion.

As money and other assistance poured in from around the country, Chicago began rebuilding. The **Chicago Relief and Aid Society** helped residents build new houses, receive health care, and find jobs. Businesses set up temporary offices, while construction workers began work on more than two hundred new buildings. Strict building codes and fire laws were passed, and most of the new construction was made of fireproof stone and brick. Chicago would never look the same—or face as much danger—ever again.

While most Americans were reading about the Great Chicago Fire, another even more destructive firestorm blazed about 250 miles to the north.

Peshtigo, Wisconsin, inhabited by two thousand people, was a small town on the banks of the Peshtigo River that was surrounded by thick pine forests. The town was home to a sawmill and a factory that made shingles, wooden pails, and broom handles.

It was a dry year in 1871, and no rain had fallen for over three months. Despite the dry conditions, many small fires were deliberately set in the woods. Some were started by railroad workers clearing land for new tracks or farmers burning tree stumps to clear land for farming. Others were set by hunters and trappers. On October 8, a strong wind combined several of these smaller blazes into one large fire and sent it racing through the forest.

By Sunday night, the air in Peshtigo was thick with smoke and unbearably hot. Then, a strange roaring filled the air as the fire swept through the town. The fire consumed all the oxygen in the air, making it impossible to breathe. Eyewitnesses described people bursting into flames as they tried to outrun the fire. Every building in Peshtigo burned down, and the entire town was destroyed in an hour.

Terrified evacuees raced toward the river, desperately searching for an escape. A Catholic priest, **Father Peter Pernin**, later wrote that "The banks of the river as far as the eye could reach were covered with people standing there, motionless as statues, some with eyes staring upturned toward heaven and tongues protruded." But even the river wasn't safe. The wind was so strong that it drove the flames right over the water. For several hours, the people in the river had to throw water over themselves to keep from burning to death. Finally, the fire moved through Peshtigo and headed across the state line into Michigan, where it caused even more damage.

Father Pernin described the horrible scene in Peshtigo after the fire: "Of the houses, trees, fences three days ago, nothing whatever remained, save a few blackened posts still standing." The toll on animals and people was also horribly evident. The burned bodies of cattle and other animals lay throughout the area, while rows of new graves marked the number of human victims.

The Peshtigo fire burned more than four million acres of land in Wisconsin and Michigan, and it destroyed twenty-three towns and villages. The blaze killed about eight hundred people in Peshtigo, and about fifteen hundred people in the entire region. It stands as the worst fire in United States history, but because it occurred on the same day as the more famous Great Chicago Fire, the Peshtigo fire has been all but forgotten.

The loudest sound ever recorded came from a small island in the middle of the ocean. This enormous roar was the worst volcanic eruption in history, and it occurred on the Indonesian island of **Krakatoa**.

In 1883, the volcanic island of Krakatoa measured about eighteen square miles and stood 2,700 feet tall. It lay in the Sunda Straits, a narrow body of water between two larger Indonesian islands of Java and Sumatra. No one lived on Krakatoa, and it was covered with a thick forest.

Krakatoa had erupted before in 1680 and 1681. After that, the island was quiet until September 1, 1880, when an earthquake struck. For the next three years, the area continued to shake. Then, on May 20, 1883, the volcano erupted, sending a huge column of ash and smoke seven miles into the air. However, this blast was nothing compared to what was still to come.

On the afternoon of August 27, a tremendous explosion rocked the island. The noise was so loud that it was heard thousands of miles away in Australia and Japan. People thought the sound had come from a ship explosion or gunfire.

Most of the island disappeared, as five cubic miles of dirt and rocks blew up into the sky. A thick cloud of dust, ash, and smoke drifted seventeen miles high. Scientists estimate that the force of the eruption was thousands of times more powerful than the atomic bombs dropped on Japan during World War II. Where a 2,700-foot-tall mountain had once stood, there was now a 980-foot-deep crater.

Although Krakatoa was uninhabited, many people lived on the islands around it. The eruption killed thirty-six thousand of these residents. Most were killed by huge tidal waves that raced across the ocean. The force of the explosion sent towering waves of water, estimated at more than hundred feet tall, rushing toward other islands. The tsunamis destroyed 300 villages over an 8,000-mile area, and ships were carried a mile up onto land. Observers in Hawaii noticed high waves, and the tide was six inches higher in San Francisco Bay.

People who survived the terrible tsunami lost their homes, possessions, and jobs. The Dutch government, which controlled Indonesia at the time, sent relief food and money to help the victims.

The effects of the eruption were felt around the world. The wind picked up the dust and ash from Krakatoa's explosion and carried it around the planet. There was so much dust, in fact, that it blocked out some sunlight. For the next two years, until the dust finally settled, the sky was darker and the weather was cooler. The dust did create beautiful sunsets, though, and the sun and moon appeared to be different colors.

Krakatoa remained active after the huge explosion of 1883. An eruption in 1927 created a new volcano inside the crater formed by the 1883 explosion. Residents named this mountain **Anak Krakatoa**, or "Son of Krakatoa." Today, people still live on nearby islands, watching carefully and hoping that the volcano never explodes with as much force as it did in 1883.

By early March 1888, the people in the American Northeast were ready for spring. However, winter was about to return with a vengeance.

On Sunday, March 11, heavy rains drenched New York City. Shortly after midnight, the air turned frigid, and the rain turned into snow. For the next fifteen hours, snow fell as fast as an inch an hour. The blizzard—a combination of heavy snow, high winds, and very cold temperatures—covered the Northeast from Maine all the way down to Maryland. Temperatures dropped as low as –5°F as twenty-one inches of snow buried New York City. And other cities received much more snow—up to fifty-five inches in Troy, New York!

New York City, along with other major cities, was paralyzed by the blizzard. Huge snowdrifts stopped trains and blocked streets. Many city trains ran on elevated tracks, but the rails became so icy that the trains could not move, trapping fifteen thousand riders high above the streets. Horse-drawn streetcars and cabs were pulled off the streets because the horses could not walk through the deep snow.

Some people tried to walk through the drifting snow, only to be blown over by the wind or collapse from exhaustion and cold. New York City police officers rescued hundreds of people buried in snowdrifts up to ten feet high. Sadly, at least two hundred people froze to death in New York City, and a total of eight hundred died on the East Coast.

The storm also proved deadly at sea. The wind blew as hard as 90 mph, whipping the water into huge waves. About two hundred ships either sank or were wrecked, and at least one hundred sailors were killed.

The snow and ice also brought down telephone and telegraph wires. Cities were isolated with no way to communicate with the outside world.

The snow finally stopped on Tuesday morning. A newspaper in Vermont described the scene: "No paths, no streets, no sidewalks, no lights, no roads, no guests, no calls, no teams, no hacks, no trains, no moon, no meat, no milk, no paper, no mail, no news, no thing [sic]—but snow."

Residents spent the next few days tunneling through drifts, shoveling their way out of their houses and repairing roofs and awnings that had been damaged by the storm. Work crews removed tons of snow from city streets and dumped it in the river. This was a massive job in the days before snowplows and heavy trucks because workers had nothing except shovels and carts.

The Great Blizzard of 1888 encouraged cities to think of new ways to set up communication and transportation systems so they would not be damaged by storms. Many cities, including New York, began running telephone and power lines underground, where they were protected from high winds and heavy snow. In 1897, Boston became the first American city to introduce a subway system for underground transportation. And residents of the Northeast kept their shovels handy just in case another blizzard came along!

Some floods are caused by natural events, such as heavy rain. Others are caused by human carelessness. The **Johnstown flood** was a combination of both.

The spring of 1889 had been unusually wet in Pennsylvania's Conemaugh Valley. The ten thousand residents of Johnstown were worried about a nearby lake called Lake Conemaugh, also called the **South Fork Dam**. The lake had been created to provide recreation for members of the South Fork Fishing and Hunting Club, and it held about twenty million tons of water. At the time that the club was chartered, the dam holding back the water had been rebuilt, but building regulations were not followed properly and the dam was poorly designed.

On the night of May 30, eight inches of rain fell in the Conemaugh Valley. The water level in Lake Conemaugh rose three feet during the night, and the water had almost reached the top of the dam by morning. Workers began piling dirt on top of the dam wall in hopes of holding the water back. Others tried to widen a spillway to safely release some of the water, but it was no use.

At 3:10 p.m., the dam gave way. Twenty million tons of water poured into the valley, and the entire lake was emptied within forty minutes.

As the flood raced toward Johnstown, it destroyed several smaller towns in its path and killed twenty-two passengers on a train. Then, it buried Johnstown under ten to thirty feet of water. Buildings washed away or collapsed under the tremendous force.

Every tree in the town park was uprooted and carried away. "I could see houses going down before it [the water] like a child's play blocks set on edge in a row," said a survivor named Richard Davis. "As it came nearer, I could see houses totter for a moment, then rise, and the next moment be crushed like eggshells against each other."

People struggled to survive the force of the water. Some clutched onto pieces of debris and held on for dear life as the water swept them along. Others ran for higher ground. The water left a trail of wreckage behind it. Some of this debris caught fire, killing hundreds more.

More than twenty-two hundred people died in the flood. The town was leveled to huge piles of mud and wreckage, including rocks, trees, train cars, machinery, and pieces of houses. Dead people and animals lay everywhere.

Survivors were in desperate need of food, fresh water, and shelter. The **American Red Cross** rushed in to help and the **National Guard** set up tent cities and maintain order. Within two years, Johnstown was almost completely rebuilt.

The Johnstown flood led to reforms in dam construction and safety inspections. The **U.S. Army Corps of Engineers** began working on flood control projects to protect communities around the country by raising riverbanks and widening and dredging rivers. The South Fork Dam was turned into a national park, where residents and visitors could continue to remember those who perished that day.

Today, meteorologists can forecast where a storm is headed and when it is likely to strike. However, in 1900, the city of **Galveston, Texas**, was completely unprepared for the worst natural disaster in American history.

Galveston is located on an island in the **Gulf of Mexico**. In 1900, most of the island sat just five feet above sea level. Residents were used to floods, so they were not overly concerned on September 4, when word came that a tropical storm over Cuba was heading east toward the gulf. The **National Weather Bureau** initially thought that the storm would hit Florida. However, by September 7, it veered east and was barreling toward Galveston.

Isaac Cline, the chief of the Weather Bureau's Galveston office, and his brother, **Joseph**, *were* worried. They posted a warning flag to tell everyone that a powerful storm was coming.

By the next morning, the Gulf of Mexico had risen and covered many residents' yards. Isaac drove along the beach in a horse-drawn cart, warning people to evacuate the area and retreat to higher ground. However, many people stayed on the beach, eager to watch the powerful waves—which soon drowned many of the onlookers.

By midafternoon, half of Galveston was flooded, and all the bridges connecting Galveston to the mainland had been swept away. The entire island was under four to ten feet of water. Winds swirling at 120 mph ripped roofs off houses and flung debris throughout the city. The rising water even

unearthed coffins from cemeteries and sent them floating down the streets.

As the wind, rain, and waves destroyed everything in their path, survivors clung desperately to pieces of wood, trees, and buildings in the water. Many drowned in huge waves or were killed by flying debris. Others died when the churches, hospitals, and other buildings where they had sought shelter collapsed.

The storm raged until about two o'clock in the morning of September 9. After it was over, Joseph Cline described the scene: "Dreadful sights met our gaze on all sides... We climbed over dead bodies sprawled and piled where the flood had left them, and over heaps of wreckage. Debris from four to ten feet deep and extending for blocks packed with dead was all that was left of thousands of homes and the human beings who had lived in them one day earlier."

More than six thousand people died in the disaster, and tens of thousands were left homeless. One eyewitness described the city as "a complete wreck."

Galveston learned from the terrible storm. The city constructed a 17-foot-high seawall and dumped tons of sand behind it to raise the city's elevation. The Weather Bureau appointed Isaac Cline as director of the nation's first scientific study of hurricanes to improve storm forecasting and tracking. These actions saved lives in future natural disasters and showed everyone how important it was to be prepared when a storm is on the way.

For hundreds of years, people had lived in Saint-Pierre, a port city in the shadow of **Mount Pelée**. This 4,430-foot-high volcano, located on the Caribbean island of Martinique, had only a few minor eruptions since the early 1700s. All that changed, however, on May 8, 1902.

In April, smoke and ash began falling from the mountain, and a small earthquake rumbled. Poisonous gas from the volcano suffocated animals in

Saint-Pierre and made many residents sick. "The rain of ashes never ceases," a local newspaper reported.

The ashes also sent swarms of insects and snakes into the city. At least fifty people and two hundred animals died from snakebites. Despite these danger signs, city officials assured everyone that they were safe, and even sent soldiers to guard the roads to prevent residents from evacuating.

On May 5, lava poured out of the side of Mount Pelée. It flowed down the mountain and destroyed a sugar refinery, killing thirty workers inside. Still, officials minimized the public's worries.

Then, at 7:50 a.m. on May 8, Mount Pelée erupted. A huge cloud of hot steam and lava burst out of the volcano at 300 mph. Unlike some other types of volcanic eruptions, Mount Pelée oozed a hot lava and ash slurry down its sides instead of shooting lava from its top.

The force of the blast thrust huge boulders high into the air. Worst of all, the blast released a cloud of superhot, poisonous gas that instantly suffocated everyone in its path. After the gas passed over the city, air rushed in, and everything burst into flames. Within three minutes, thirty-four thousand people—including almost every resident of Saint-Pierre and many sailors on ships in the harbor—were dead. One eyewitness on a ship said, "...on shore, I saw men and women rushing back and forth amid the flames. Then came that choking smoke, and they would drop like dead flies."

Only two residents of Saint-Pierre survived the disaster. One was a man who managed to escape the city during the eruption. The other survivor was August Ciparis, who had been convicted of murder and sentenced to death. He was in a dungeon cell with thick walls and only a tiny, barred window for air. The eruption sent a wave of heat into Ciparis's cell, burning his back and legs. However, the walls of the dungeon protected him from the poisonous gas. Four days later, a rescue team found Ciparis and brought him to a hospital. He was later pardoned of his crime and set free.

Mount Pelée continued to erupt for several months, destroying the few buildings that were still standing after the initial disaster. An explosion on May 20 killed two thousand more, including relief workers bringing supplies to the island.

When the volcano finally quieted, scientists came to study the mountain and learned many new things about volcanic eruptions. Today, a volcanic eruption that sends destructive pyroclastic flows down its sides is known as a "Pelean eruption."

The day began as a pleasant excursion for a German church group, but it ended in a horrifying nightmare as a deadly fire consumed the **PS *General Slocum*** and almost everyone on board.

The *General Slocum* was built in 1891, and for thirteen years, the steamboat sailed around New York Harbor, carrying passengers between lower Manhattan and the beaches of Rockaway several miles away. On June 15, 1904, more than thirteen hundred members of St. Mark's Evangelical Lutheran Church boarded the *General Slocum* to attend the annual church picnic.

The passengers had no idea that the *General Slocum* was extremely unsafe. Just five weeks before the accident, the ship had passed a safety inspection, but it was later revealed that the inspector had barely looked at any of the fire equipment on board. If he had, he would have noticed that the life preservers were from 1891, and the cork that made them float had rotted away to dust. Also, the lifeboats were stuck to the ceiling due to a thick coat of paint, and the crew had never conducted a fire drill.

The night before the picnic, men from the church delivered three barrels of glasses packed in hay. After the glasses were unpacked, a deckhand stored the hay-filled barrels in the forward cabin. Later, another deckhand spilled oil on the hay when he was lighting lamps. The boat was barely underway on the morning of June 15 when the oil-soaked hay burst into flames. The fresh coat of paint on the ship fueled the fire, boiling off the walls with intense heat.

People on shore watched in horror as the ship sailed up the East River with flames and smoke pouring out of the forward cabin. **Captain William Van Schaick** finally beached the burning ship on North Brother Island in the middle of the river. By then, passengers had discovered that the life preservers and lifeboats were useless. People jumped into the river, only to drown in the rough currents.

Within twenty minutes, the *General Slocum* was a burned-out hulk. The final death toll amounted to 1,021 people, making it the worst maritime disaster in New York City's history. The city's German community was devastated. On Friday, June 17, there were 114 funerals at St. Mark's Church alone.

An investigation into the disaster revealed that the crew and the captain were poorly trained, and the steamboat's owner and inspector were to be held liable for their negligence. Although a grand jury indicted the captain, first mate, inspector, and several officers of the steamboat company, only Captain Van Schaick was ultimately convicted of not holding fire drills or properly training the crew. He was sentenced to ten years in prison but served only three-and-a-half years before he was pardoned by President William Howard Taft.

The remains of the *General Slocum* were converted into a barge, which sank near Atlantic City during a storm in 1911. After the disaster, excursion ships faced stricter safety standards, preventing future family outings from ending in tragedy.

◆ Forty seconds can seem like a lifetime. That's how residents of San Francisco felt early in the morning of April 18, 1906, as their city began to shake and would not stop.

The earthquake struck at 5:12 a.m. when many residents were sleeping. For forty seconds, the ground rolled and shook. Then, after a brief pause, came another, even more powerful tremor, measuring 7.9 on the Richter scale. The quake's epicenter was near San Francisco's Golden Gate Bridge and occurred when a section of rock moved along the **San Andreas Fault.**

Thousands of buildings collapsed. Many were poorly built, flimsy, wooden houses resting on landfill. But even large, sturdy buildings, such as City Hall and the Valencia Hotel, slid into the street or toppled like dominoes. Hundreds were killed as buildings fell on top of them.

Streets were ripped open, and streetcar lines twisted from the force of the quake. Roads were littered with broken glass and chunks of brick and stone. People fled their homes, only to be struck and killed by falling debris. Others died when the ground opened up beneath them, ultimately crushing them to death.

One survivor, W. E. Alexander, described the experience: "My feelings were like what I suppose a rat's are when vigorously shaken by a terrier and then slammed down on the ground." Another eyewitness, Sam Wolfe, wrote: "The street seemed to move like waves of water. On my way down Market Street, the whole side of a building fell out and came so near me that I was covered and blinded by the dust."

The earthquake also ripped open natural gas and electrical lines, causing an even greater disaster. Within a few minutes of the quake, at least fifty fires were burning in the city. Because water mains were also destroyed, there was no way to extinguish them. Firefighters dynamited many buildings in an effort to create firebreaks, but their efforts caused more destruction and did little to stop the fires. It took three days to get the fires under control, and by then, half of San Francisco had been razed to the ground. Meanwhile, looters filled the streets, and soldiers were sent in with shoot-on-sight orders.

The earthquake and fires killed more than twenty-five hundred people. They destroyed more than twenty-eight thousand buildings and left two hundred twenty-five thousand people homeless. Tent cities sprang up in parks to house refugees and some resorted to sleeping on sidewalks. Relief centers were opened to provide food and fresh water, and money and supplies poured into the city from all over the country.

Within a week, some businesses had reopened, and people were starting to rebuild their lives. By 1909, almost twenty thousand new homes had been built. These buildings were constructed to withstand earthquakes, in the hopes that San Francisco would never again experience such devastation.

Mining is one of the most dangerous occupations in the world. Miners work deep underground, digging coal and other valuable minerals out of rock and earth. They are in constant danger of fires, floods, poisonous gases, and cave-ins. In the early twentieth century, hundreds of miners died in accidents every year. One of the deadliest mine disasters occurred in the small town of **Monongah, West Virginia.**

By 1907, West Virginia was the third-leading coal producer in the United States. The Monongah coal mine was owned and operated by the **Fairmont Coal Company**, one of the largest companies in the world. On December 7, 1906, a full shift of workers was working in shafts No. 6 and No. 8 in the mines, which were connected deep underground.

At 10:28 a.m., a young coal miner was guiding a train of coal cars out of the mine, when suddenly, the metal coupling that held two of the cars together broke. The cars behind the broken coupling rolled backward into the No. 6 shaft, right toward a wall full of electrical cables.

The young miner ran toward the opening of the tunnel, hoping to reach the switches and cut off the electricity before it was too late. But before he could reach the switches, the train hit the wall and severed the cables. Sparks flew and ignited the methane gas inside the tunnel. A tremendous blast roared through shaft No. 6 and spread to the

A monument dedicated to the lost miners

connecting shaft No. 8. The explosion was heard eight miles away and sent the walls and ceilings of the tunnels crashing down on the miners.

The force of the explosion blew the young miner right out of the tunnel. He was lucky. Three hundred sixty-six other workers were trapped in the blazing mine behind him. Although rescuers and townspeople raced to the scene, there was so much fire coming out of the mine entrance that no one could get inside to help potential survivors.

A few hours later, a small miracle occurred. Four bloodied men, battered and coughing from the poisonous fumes, crawled out of the No. 8 shaft. They had been working near the mine entrance and were able to reach the shaft's opening before the tunnel caved in behind them. They were the only survivors.

It was five days before rescuers could enter the mine. They found no survivors—only crushed and burned bodies. In all, 362 men died in the Monongah mines. Ironically, one of the deceased was an insurance agent who had gone in to sell life insurance to miners. It took rescuers several weeks to find all the bodies.

The Monongah tragedy brought new calls for mining safety. West Virginia swiftly outlawed connected underground mines, and three years later in 1910, the United States government established the **U.S. Bureau of Mines** to regulate and improve safety conditions in mines nationwide.

A building crowded with hundreds of workers, few escape routes, and a fast-moving fire. These were the ingredients for a tragedy that touched the lives of working women all over New York City.

The **Triangle Shirtwaist Factory** employed about five hundred women to sew blouses. Most were Russian and Italian immigrants between the ages of thirteen and twenty-two. The factory was so crowded that the young women could hardly move. Aside from the building's one fire escape, the four elevators and two narrow staircases were the only ways out.

At 4:45 p.m. on March 25, someone on the eighth floor spotted a fire in a basket of rags under a sewing machine. The blaze spread quickly, fed by bits of cloth and paper patterns scattered everywhere. Two hundred young workers, screaming in panic, rushed for the elevators and the stairs.

One stairway door was locked. The other door opened inward, and it became impossible to pull it open against the crowd pressing against it. A few women escaped by breaking a glass panel in the door, but most perished in the fire.

The fire spread to the ninth and tenth floors, trapping hundreds more workers. Some were able to escape in the elevator. Elevator operator Joseph Zito recalled, "The girls fought each other to get in. I made about twenty trips in all, I think... On the last few trips I could see the fire... spurting out from the elevator doors on the ninth and the tenth floors."

Zito had just completed his last trip when falling bodies sent the elevator crashing to the bottom of the shaft. "The bodies kept on plunging down... Some of their clothing was burning as they fell, and I could see streaks of fire coming down like rockets."

By the time firefighters arrived, workers were jumping out of windows to escape the blaze, only to be killed when they hit the pavement. Others climbed down the fire escape, but it collapsed under the weight. Fire ladders were too short to reach above the sixth floor of the ten-story building. By the time the blaze was extinguished, just 18 minutes later, 145 people had died.

Although city officials were aware that many factories were firetraps, owners refused to improve conditions because they did not want to cut into profits. A strike by workers the year before had not changed anything either. After the fire, reporter William Shepherd wrote, "I remembered their great strike of last year, in which these same girls had demanded more sanitary conditions and safety precautions in the shops. These dead bodies were the answer."

Although the Triangle Shirtwaist Factory owners were cleared of any wrongdoing, the fire did have a lasting effect. **Labor unions**, such as the **International Ladies' Garment Workers' Union (ILGWU)**, became popular because of the tragedy and grew to be powerful forces in winning better working conditions. New York City instituted fire and factory **safety codes** in October 1911, and the rest of the country soon followed suit.

It was a clear, cold night on the northern portion of the Atlantic Ocean on April 14, 1912. The **luxury liner Royal Mail Ship (RMS)** *Titanic* was on its maiden voyage from England to the United States. Suddenly, a lookout cried, "Iceberg, right ahead!"

The ship's engines stopped, and it veered to port to miss the iceberg. Sixteen watertight bulkheads inside the ship slammed closed. The *Titanic*'s designers originally bragged that these bulkheads made the ship unsinkable, but they were wrong.

The iceberg brushed against the side of the ship, ripping open five of the watertight compartments. Water rushed into the front of the ship. Then it flooded over the top of the bulkheads and into compartment after compartment. The *Titanic* began to sink.

Telegraph operators sent a distress call to other ships. Unfortunately, most were too far away to reach the *Titanic* in time. Others had already turned off their telegraphs for the night and didn't receive the message.

Crew members ordered passengers into lifeboats. However, there were not enough for everyone on board. British law required all ships over 10,000 tons to carry sixteen lifeboats. The *Titanic* weighed 46,328 tons. Even though the vessel actually had more boats than what the law required, there were only enough to accommodate half of the 2,207 passengers. Even worse, many lifeboats were only half full when they set off away from the ship. By the time the second-class and third-class passengers reached the deck, most of the lifeboats had departed.

Because crew members ordered "Women and children first" to fill the lifeboats, most of the first-class men were also not allowed on. Some of the richest and most famous men in the world went down with the ship, including business tycoon **John Jacob Astor**, philanthropist **Benjamin Guggenheim**, Broadway theater owner and producer **Henry B. Harris**, and **Isidor Straus**, co-owner of Macy's Department Store.

At 2:15 a.m., the *Titanic* tilted almost straight up in the water. The lights flickered off, and a terrible crashing sound came from inside the ship as furniture, dishes, and cargo tumbled loose. Then, the *Titanic* disappeared beneath the surface.

Around 4:00 a.m., **RMS** *Carpathia* appeared and rescued 685 survivors floating in lifeboats, but 1,522 passengers and crew members died in the disaster.

News of the *Titanic*'s sinking shocked the world. People were heartbroken at the loss of so many lives and astonished that the "unsinkable" *Titanic* had such a terrible fate on its first voyage.

The *Titanic* disaster led to changes in the industry. Ships were required to carry enough lifeboats for every passenger and crew member. Telegraph operators stayed on duty all night so they could answer any distress messages. Shipping routes were moved farther south to avoid icebergs, and government boats began patrolling the North Atlantic for dangerous icebergs. Any ships traveling through areas with icebergs were instructed to slow down or change course to avoid accidents. Meanwhile, the *Titanic* remains two and a half miles beneath the surface as an eerie memorial to the 1,522 lives lost that day.

The **Stag Cañon Fuel Company** owned and operated a coal mine in Dawson, New Mexico. The mine was considered a model of safety and Stag Cañon was seen as one of the best mining companies in the United States. It had all the cutting-edge safety devices of the time. Electric fans circulated fresh air and prevented the buildup of poisonous methane gas. Sprayers in the shafts wet down the coal dust to prevent explosions. Electricity triggered from outside the mine was used to set off dynamite that freed chunks of coal from the shafts. But despite all these precautions, the Stag Cañon Mine turned into a deathtrap on October 22, 1913.

Dynamite was considered a safe and efficient way to loosen coal deposits. Explosions were carefully controlled and monitored. However, when workers set off a series of dynamite blasts at three o'clock in the afternoon, something went terribly wrong. No one ever found out why, but the dynamite set off an unplanned explosion that ignited coal dust in the mines. The main shaft of the mine collapsed from the blast, trapping 284 miners deep underground. One of the trapped men was the general superintendent of the mine, Frank McDermott.

The explosion also destroyed the circulating fans. Without them, poisonous gases built up inside the mine, quickly filling the tunnels and killing many men. The gases were so strong that when a rescue team entered the shaft two hours later wearing full protective gear, they were overcome by the fumes and had to be rescued by another team. Workers—including workers from other mines—pumped fresh air into the shaft. Along with making the shaft safe for rescue workers, they also hoped that the air would help trapped miners stay alive long enough to be rescued.

Five hours after the explosions, rescuers were finally able to enter the collapsed mine shaft. Although they had hoped that some men had escaped through an air shaft, the blast had sealed all exits. Rescuers found only twenty-one survivors. Two hundred sixty-three other workers, including Superintendent McDermott, had been killed. Rescuers piled their bodies in carts used to take coal out of the mine, and solemnly brought them up to the surface. The bodies were identified and met by family members, who had set up a vigil outside the mine as they prayed for good news about their husbands, fathers, sons, and brothers trapped far below.

The Stag Cañon Mine continued to operate after the disaster. Ten years later, in February 1923, tragedy struck the mine again, when another explosion killed 120 miners.

Ships are often loaded with very dangerous things. When two ships collided in one Canadian harbor in 1917, it set off the worst accidental explosions in history.

Halifax was once a bustling port city on the eastern coast of Canada. It was especially busy during World War I as an embarkation point for ships crossing the Atlantic Ocean in convoys.

At 9:00 a.m. on December 6, the French freighter **Steamship (SS) Mont-Blanc** arrived in

The explosion created a huge pyrocumulus cloud above Halifax

Halifax from New York. She was filled to capacity with eight million tons of dynamite and a flammable chemical called benzene.

As the *Mont-Blanc* moved through a half-mile-wide channel called **The Narrows**, another ship suddenly appeared in front of it. Empty Belgian relief ship **SS *Imo*** was heading straight toward the French freighter!

The *Mont-Blanc*'s captain gave orders for the ship to stay on course and try to pass the *Imo*. However, the *Imo*'s captain reversed engines to stop his ship. Because the *Imo* was empty, the motion of reversing the engines caused the front of the ship to swing toward the *Mont-Blanc* and collide with the fully loaded freighter. The compartment filled with benzene instantly caught fire.

The *Mont-Blanc*'s captain knew that when the fire reached the dynamite, the ship would effectively become a bomb. He called the fire department and ordered his men to "Abandon ship!" Sailors rushed to the docks and ran to the hills. The crews of other ships also raced away from the scene, along with workers at factories around the harbor.

Seventeen minutes later, the *Mont-Blanc* exploded. Pieces of metal and sheets of fire blanketed the city. A huge wall of water ripped ships from their moorings and flung them onto the shore. Hurricane-force winds roared through the neighborhood of Richmond, destroying a two-and-a-half-mile area of the town. The **Intercolonial Railway Station** collapsed, trapping hundreds of early morning commuters inside. The **American Sugar Refining Company**, which was located near the docks, was destroyed and one hundred workers there perished. Local schools also collapsed, killing almost five hundred fifty children.

Fire quickly spread through Halifax, but there was no one left to fight it. The city's firefighters, who had just arrived at the scene, all lay dead from the blast. However, an hour after the explosion, heavy snow began to fall, extinguishing the fires and saving what was left of the city. Another fortunate event occurred when a tidal wave swept over a naval ammunitions factory near The Narrows, preventing it from also catching fire.

The explosion killed more than twelve hundred people, injured nine thousand, and left twenty-five thousand residents homeless. Soon after the disaster, rumors spread that it was an act of war caused by German spies. However, the collision was ultimately ruled an accident. Halifax was rebuilt and again served as Canada's most important naval port during World War II.

Since 1904, the ground beneath New York City's streets has rumbled with subway trains, carrying thousands of people around the city. These tunnels have also been the scene of several disasters, most notably one particular terrible crash in **Brooklyn** in 1918.

That year, old wooden subway cars were being replaced with stronger steel coaches. However, a **Brooklyn Rapid Transit (BRT)** train heading toward the **Malbone Tunnel** in Brooklyn on November 1 was still using the flimsy wooden cars. That afternoon, the cars were packed with office workers, most of whom were women, and families returning from some leisurely shopping.

The train operator, **Edward Anthony Luciano**, was not in the best shape that day. He had just gotten over the Spanish influenza and was mourning the loss of his toddler, who had died just days before. Luciano was actually trained to be a train dispatcher, not a train operator. However, other BRT operators had gone on strike that day, and Luciano was working overtime to fill in for the missing crew.

As the five-car train approached the Malbone Tunnel, it was traveling about 30 mph, well over the speed limit of 6 mph. Luciano tried to slow the train, but the brakes were defective. Instead of slowing down, the train gained speed. When it reached a curve before the tunnel entrance, the first car derailed and crashed into the tunnel wall. That car was destroyed, and the other cars piled up behind it, completely filling the tracks with twisted debris.

The crash caused the ancient wooden coaches to smash into each other and splinter into pieces. Riders were crushed as the train cars collapsed, and many were impaled by sharp stakes that had once been the walls and flooring of the train cars. Others were killed when the wrecked cars burst into flames.

Firefighters, police officers, and ambulance workers rushed to the scene, but they had a hard time reaching the train, which was in a narrow area between steep concrete walls. First responders used ladders from firetrucks to carry out the injured and the dead. Unfortunately, there were not enough ambulances to handle all the victims, so private cars were also pressed into service.

The train operator, Edward Luciano, survived the crash and was accused of recklessness and incompetence. "He had no right to be running this train," said the Brooklyn district attorney. Brooklyn's mayor also threatened to charge BRT officials with manslaughter for not settling the strike and allowing unqualified workers to run the trains. Although Luciano was charged with manslaughter, a jury found him not guilty.

Approximately one hundred passengers died in the crash, making it the worst subway disaster in U.S. history. Less than two months later, the Brooklyn Rapid Transit Company went bankrupt. However, the crash did lead to the replacement of all wooden coaches with stronger steel coaches—a decision that probably saved countless lives in future accidents.

In 1918, Americans were fighting in World War I, when millions of people also entered a battle with another deadly enemy—a novel virus strain.

In March, American soldiers training at an army camp in Kansas fell ill due to a virus that results in **influenza**, or the flu. Symptoms included a high fever, chills, coughing, sneezing, body aches, and nosebleeds. Their skin often turned bluish from a lack of oxygen.

Most people catch the flu several times in their lives and recover completely. Usually, only the elderly and very young children die from influenza due to their weakened or undeveloped immune systems. But this influenza was killing strong, young people. Autopsies on soldiers in Kansas showed that the men's lungs were filled with bloody froth and mucus, meaning that victims literally drowned in their own fluids.

More influenza outbreaks struck army camps around the country. Then the disease spread to camps in Europe, presumably introduced by American soldiers sent there to fight in World War I. Soon, soldiers and citizens in England, France, Germany, Spain, Norway, New Zealand, and several African nations were dying from the disease.

When soldiers returned to the States after the war ended in November 1918, the flu came back with them. Outbreaks struck most major cities throughout the nation, and even **President Woodrow Wilson** fell ill.

Philadelphia was the hardest-hit American city. It closed all schools, churches, theaters, and other public gathering places. However, people still spread influenza as they rode on streetcars and trains or worked in crowded factories and offices. By the middle of October, seven thousand people had died.

It was impossible to live a normal life with so many people sick and dying. Police officers and firefighters were too sick to protect citizens. Garbage was strewn everywhere because there were no sanitation workers to collect it. Hospitals were overwhelmed with patients, and there was a shortage of doctors and nurses to care for the sick. Even worse, people were dying faster than they could be buried, and dead bodies began piling up in morgues. By early November, the pandemic was over in Philadelphia, but almost twelve thousand had died of the disease or related infections.

Other cities had multiple outbreaks. More than thirty-five hundred people died in two outbreaks in San Francisco between October 1918 and January 1919. People wore masks, avoided public gatherings, and tried all sorts of home remedies, but nothing could slow the spread.

By 1920, the pandemic had ended and between twenty and forty million people around the world had died. Approximately 675,000 people died in total in the United States.

The 1918 influenza **pandemic** taught scientists a lot about diseases, how they spread, and how to control them. Today, vaccination programs and other medical breakthroughs help manage outbreaks. However, it is still much too easy for new diseases to spread throughout cities, whole nations, or even the world, as evidenced by the **COVID-19 pandemic** that the world experienced a century later. Unfortunately, pandemics are a threat that will never completely disappear.

All disasters are terrifying and tragic, but some can also be just plain weird! When a neighborhood in Boston was devastated by a flood of sticky **molasses**, the event became one of the strangest disasters in history.

The **Purity Distillery** was located in Boston's North End near the Charles River. The company had a 58-foot-tall, 90-foot-wide tank that was used to store molasses. Shortly after noon on January 15, 1919, the tank was filled with more than two million gallons.

Without warning, the tank suddenly blew apart, unleashing a flood of sticky, syrupy goo. The deluge rushed through the distillery's yard and into the streets. The 8-foot-high wave, moving about 35 mph, shattered buildings and sent railroad cars flying through the air. Workers at the distillery and nearby buildings were caught in the gooey tide. The force of the molasses was so strong that it knocked buildings right off their foundations. Many people drowned or were smothered in the molasses while others were killed by falling debris or collapsing buildings.

The molasses also destroyed the tank itself. Huge steel plates flew in all directions. One hit the girders of an elevated railway line and snapped its steel supports. The track collapsed down to the street. Fortunately, a train had just cleared the tracks before the collapse. Another train was able to stop before it reached the disaster.

Firemen and other rescuers hurried to pull victims out of the sweet, sticky flood. Twenty-one people and many horses were killed. Another fifteen hundred people were injured. Cars, wagons, and carts lay shattered in the streets, along with the remains of houses and other buildings.

Cleaning the streets proved to be an unusual challenge because the molasses was so sticky. Firefighters had to wade through several feet of molasses. They used hoses to wash the molasses off buildings and streets and into the gutters, where it finally flowed into the Charles River. As people walked through the devastated area, the molasses got on their shoes and clothes, then spread to other areas of the city. Everything was sticky, from sidewalks and public telephones to seats on the trains. The air smelled like molasses for years afterward.

At first, the disaster was blamed on an explosion in the tank, which many speculated was caused by molasses fermenting and emitting powerful gases. The Purity Distilling Company claimed that a bomb had been placed in the tank by "enemies of the United States."

However, after six years, many lawsuits, and the testimonies of three thousand witnesses, an investigation revealed that the tank had not been built correctly. The steel walls were too thin, and a manhole cover in the bottom of the tank was not strong enough to withstand the pressure of the molasses inside. The tank's owners paid almost $1 million in damages.

The Boston Daily Globe EXTRA

VOL XCV – NO. 16   BOSTON, THURSDAY MORNING, JANUARY 16, 1919 -SIXTEEN PAGES   PRICE TWO CENTS

MOLASSES TANK EXPLOSION
INJURES 50 AND KILLS 11

SCENE OF RUIN AND DESOLATION IN NORTH END AFTER DESTRUCTION OF PURITY DISTILLING COMPANY TANK AND NEARBY STRUCTURES

Death and Devastation In Wake of North End Disaster

Buildings Demolished, Sticky Mass Flood Streets—Loss $500,000

Red Cross Women, Firemen and Sailors Do Heroic Work In Aiding Victims

LIST OF DEAD
DEAD AT NORTH GROVE STREET MORSE

Although tornadoes can do tremendous damage, the devastation is usually limited to a small area. However, in 1925, one **tornado** roared through three states, causing death and destruction for hundreds of miles.

It was a warm and humid day in the Midwestern part of the United States on March 18, 1925. Thunderstorms were brewing, and one of these storms turned into a killer as a funnel cloud first touched ground in

Annapolis, Missouri, around one o'clock in the afternoon. Eleven people died before the storm, moving at 60 mph, raced across the Mississippi River into the state of Illinois. Unlike most tornadoes, the funnel was so close to the ground that people did not see it coming. Eyewitnesses described the storm as a "black fog."

Ninety people were killed and two hundred were injured in Gorham, Illinois, which was leveled by the tornado. The same thing happened in nearby Murphysboro. More than one hundred fifty blocks in the two-hundred-block city were destroyed, and 234 people were killed. The tornado tipped over many coal- and wood-burning stoves, starting fires that left eight thousand people homeless.

The storm moved on to DeSoto, Illinois, where it blew apart wooden houses. More than one hundred people were killed, many impaled by splinters of wood. A resident named F. M. Hewitt described the storm as a "seething, boiling mass of clouds whose color constantly changed. From the upper portion

came a roaring noise as of many trains. Below this cloud was a tapering dark cloud mass reaching earthward." Tragically, the storm ripped through the town's school, killing eighty-eight students and teachers.

The tornado was not over yet. It lifted a railroad bridge right off its concrete foundation near Zeigler, Illinois, and destroyed sixty-four houses in two minutes. The force of the wind drove a wooden plank into a tree and tore down telephone lines. Cars and pieces of buildings were carried for miles. A school was destroyed, but the sixteen students inside were picked up and put down, uninjured, 150 yards away.

Next, the tornado moved through Indiana. It destroyed the town of Griffin and heavily damaged another town called Princeton. Buildings were demolished, and a car was ripped into pieces and scattered for miles.

Finally, at 4:18 p.m., the tornado disappeared. It had killed 689 people, injured 2,000 more, and left 15,000 people homeless. It was the worst tornado in American history. The storm also had one of the longest tracks of any tornado on record, covering an astonishing 219 miles.

The residents in Missouri, Illinois, and Indiana had no warning that such a powerful storm was coming. Today, the **National Weather Service** issues tornado watches and tracks storms so residents can have a chance to seek shelter. However, tornadoes are fast and unpredictable storms, and it is still not possible to escape them all.

We usually take rain for granted. But in the Midwestern United States during the 1930s, a lack of rain turned the land into a bowl of dust.

The area called **Dust Bowl** got its name from news reporter Robert Geiger. It covered 25,000 square miles that spanned Kansas, Colorado, New Mexico, Oklahoma, and Texas. The land in this area had once been rich and prized for farming and cattle ranching. Most farmers planted wheat, because the crop could be sold for a good price. However, because wheat plants do not hold the soil well, over time the wind blew the dirt away. Cattle also damaged the ground by eating grass and breaking up the earth with their hooves.

Things got worse in 1931, when less than half the normal amount of rain and snow fell. By 1932, the ground was so dry that it turned to dust and blew away in the wind. Eyewitnesses reported 1,000-foot-high clouds that blocked out the sun like "horizontal tornadoes."

Dust soon became part of everyday life. Caroline Henderson, who lived in Oklahoma, wrote: "Dust to eat and dust to breathe and dust to drink. Dust in the beds and in the flour bin, on dishes and walls and windows, in hair and eyes and ears and teeth and throats, to say nothing of the heaped-up accumulation on floors and windowsills after one of the bad days."

April 14, 1935, became known as **Black Sunday**. The sky turned dark as tremendous dust clouds roared over Kansas, Colorado,

and Oklahoma. Traveling at 70 mph, the dust clouds dropped temperatures by fifty degrees and turned day into night. Houses, barns, fences, and cars were buried. Cattle suffocated in the dry, choking cloud. The dust produced so much static electricity that it jammed radio signals throughout the area and made metal fences and gas pumps glow.

Many people, especially babies and the elderly, suffered from "**dust pneumonia**" caused by inhaling dust and dirt all day long. People covered their faces with wet washcloths while they ate and slept to keep dust out of their mouths.

As the drought continued year after year, many farmers were left unable to pay their bills and lost their land and homes. Many of these families piled their belongings into cars and trucks and headed west, toward what they hoped would be a better life in California. The federal government gave approximately one billion dollars in aid to farmers in the area, and the economic disruption caused by Dust Bowl conditions affected the entire nation.

In 1935, the federal government created the **Soil Conservation Service** to show farmers how to plow more efficiently, grow crops that held soil and used less water, and plant trees and bushes to create windbreaks. The climate also improved, and rain began to fall again. By 1937, Dust Bowl conditions were over. However, the Midwest is still subject to droughts, and land use must be carefully managed to avoid another Dust Bowl.

A ship's crew is responsible for saving passengers during an emergency. If they fail, tragedy can result. That is the sad story of what happened on the **SS *Morro Castle*** early in the morning of September 8, 1934.

The *Morro Castle* was a luxury liner that traveled between New York City and Havana, Cuba. Despite the ship's elegance, owner company **Ward Line** paid little attention to safety. The crew never held lifeboat drills, and flammable materials were not properly stored.

At 2:45 a.m., most of the passengers and crew were sleeping when a steward opened a linen closet and saw flames. Crew members tried to put out the fire, but it quickly spread into the ventilation and elevator shafts. From there, the fire burned out the wiring and destroyed the ship's telephone and alarm systems. Crewmen alerted passengers by banging pots and pans in the hallways.

When **Captain William Warms** heard about the fire, he decided to continue toward shore, figuring he could reach Asbury Park, New Jersey, in about 30 minutes. He didn't send out an **SOS** to alert other ships or the Coast Guard, because he was afraid the Ward Company would have to pay to remove the *Morro Castle*. Finally, at 3:24 a.m., a fed-up radio operator sent his own SOS. A few minutes later, the entire electrical system on the *Morro Castle* went dead. The burning ship had no lights and no engine.

Meanwhile, most of the passengers had gathered on deck, but few had any idea what was going on. Instead of helping passengers into the lifeboats, the crew climbed on board themselves. Ninety-two of the first ninety-eight people to leave the *Morro Castle* were crewmen. Other lifeboats didn't launch at all and burned instead.

Terrified, passengers began jumping into the water. Most of these people drowned. Others were rescued hours later when the Coast Guard and a few other ships finally arrived. John Bogan, who owned a fishing boat, pulled sixty-seven people out of the water. "It was the most horrible sight I ever saw," he later told reporters. "The water was full of dead." The *Morro Castle* continued to burn until it sank into the Atlantic Ocean.

The Ward Company was sued for more than $13.5 million. Even in court, the company refused to accept responsibility for the loss of 137 lives. First, they claimed the fire was an act of God. Then they said it was an act of sabotage. Finally, they said that the ship itself had been at fault, not the crew members who abandoned the passengers.

The court did not believe any of the Ward Company's arguments. The company was found liable for the disaster and told to pay more than $1 million to settle the lawsuits.

The *Morro Castle* tragedy improved safety standards onboard ships. The United States accepted the **International Convention for Safety of Life at Sea**, which set down procedures to be followed in a disaster. Ships were also required to have sprinkler systems, and the government's safety inspection program was expanded.

During the 1930s, **airships** were the quickest and most elegant way to cross the Atlantic Ocean. The best of these ships was a German craft called the **LZ 129** *Hindenburg*, which made regular trips between Germany and Lakehurst, New Jersey. The ship was called "the queen of the skies," and was the pride of Germany's ruling **Nazi Party**. But on May 6, 1937, the *Hindenburg* became a ship of death.

The *Hindenburg* was the largest thing in the sky. The ship was 804 feet long, and as tall as a fifteen-story building. A rigid steel frame was filled with sixteen gas bags that held more than 6,992,370 cubic feet of highly flammable hydrogen. Despite its size, the *Hindenburg* weighed only 145 tons.

Because its fuel was so flammable, the crew of the *Hindenburg* took extraordinary precautions to keep the ship safe. The gas bags were tightly sealed so no gas could escape into the ship. Passengers were not allowed to smoke in most areas of the ship or even carry flash bulbs for their cameras. Because of these precautions, the *Hindenburg* had a perfect safety record.

On the evening of May 6, 1937, the *Hindenburg* prepared for a routine landing at Lakehurst. Several radio and newspaper reporters were on hand, including a reporter named Herbert Morrison from radio station WLS in Chicago. As the *Hindenburg* approached the mooring mast, Morrison began describing the scene.

Suddenly, the tail section of the ship burst into flames, which were fed by the flammable hydrogen gas that powered the ship. Within seconds, the entire ship was a mass of fire. Then the burning wreckage crashed to the ground. Thirteen passengers and twenty-two crew members died. Amazingly, sixty-two of the ninety-seven people on the ship survived.

Herb Morrison kept on broadcasting as the disaster unfolded before his eyes, even though the sight of the burning ship reduced him to tears. "It's burst into flames!... This is terrible! This is one of the worst catastrophes in the world... Oh, the humanity! Those passengers!" he sobbed. His broadcast became a classic in radio history.

Some people thought the *Hindenburg* explosion had been caused by a bomb placed on the ship in Germany by an enemy of the Nazis. However, an investigation concluded that the disaster was caused by static electricity in the air after a thunderstorm earlier that day.

Few people wanted to travel by airship after the *Hindenburg* disaster. Two years later, the Nazis plunged Europe into World War II, and travel between Germany and the United States ended. Within ten years, **airplanes** had replaced airships as the fastest way to travel.

Although the *Hindenburg* crash marked the end of an era, it also marked the beginning of a new age in communication. For the first time, thousands of people heard a big news story as it happened. Thanks to radio broadcasting, finding out what was going on in the world would never be the same.

Most **hurricanes** tend to hit the southeastern part of the United States, but a few large storms have traveled all the way up the Atlantic coast to surprise residents in **New England** and other northeastern states. Perhaps the most famous was a monster storm that hit **Long Island**, New York, and New England in late September 1938.

The 1938 hurricane began as a tropical storm near Puerto Rico. The storm hit Florida on September 19, then turned north and headed straight for Long Island. However, residents there did not expect anything more than some heavy rain. They were wrong.

The hurricane hit Long Island during the afternoon. The tide rose eighteen feet above normal, and water rushed through the streets. Telephone poles flew through the air, steeples fell from churches, and houses slid away under a 20-foot-high tidal wave. In the town of Westhampton, trees and beach houses were smashed into a pile of splintered wood. Eyewitnesses reported seeing whole houses float past with dead bodies inside. Some of the bodies had on only socks and shoes because the wind and waves had torn off all their clothing.

By nightfall, the storm had finished with Long Island and was headed for Providence, Rhode Island. The wind, blowing at more than 78 mph, tore roofs off buildings and knocked out power and telephone service. Streets flooded, sweeping up cars and people in the raging waves. Many residents were swept away by a wall of water as they struggled to board up windows and doors against the storm. A storm surge caused a wall of water to rush through the streets, covering them with almost fourteen feet of water.

Other New England communities also felt the storm's power. Four people were killed in Weare, New Hampshire, when the bridge they were standing on collapsed. A wind gust of 183 mph was recorded outside Boston. The storm destroyed many ships in the harbor of New London, Connecticut.

Harry Easton, a train engineer, wrote in *Railroad Magazine* about a nightmare trip through the storm in Connecticut: "A large hulk loomed in the darkness ahead... My heart stopped when I saw it was a house which the storm had thrown on our track... We neared the rising and falling structure until our locomotive gently touched it. The cab shivered and the windows rattled, but we kept on pushing... The hulk turned just a little and stopped. Then the gale caught the house and drove it into fast-gliding water, which carried it crazily out to sea."

By morning, all was quiet. The wind and rain had left more than six hundred people dead, including 380 victims in Rhode Island. Nine thousand homes were destroyed along with twenty-six thousand cars and more than 250 million trees. The storm caused more than $306 million in damages—an enormous sum in the 1930s. It took years for devastated communities to rebuild. And never again would New England residents think that a hurricane could not strike their homes.

It was the Saturday of Thanksgiving weekend, and the city of Boston was crowded with servicemen, college students, and other young people looking for a good time. More than eight hundred people crowded into the **Cocoanut Grove**, a popular nightclub, to dance, drink, and listen to music. But their evening of fun would quickly turn into a fiery nightmare.

A narrow stairway from the club's main floor led down to a basement area called the Melody Lounge. Couples sat in booths surrounded by a forest of artificial palm trees. No one took much notice when a busboy climbed up on a stool to replace a light bulb at 10:15 p.m. that night. Unable to see in the dark room, he lit a match, then blew it out and dropped it after he had finished his job. The smoldering match ignited a fake palm tree, creating a flash of fire.

Within seconds, the fire spread across the room, fed by the highly flammable palm trees and other decorations. Screaming people tried to escape up the narrow staircase, but the fire and smoke moved even faster. Most of the customers were trapped and died in the stairway.

Customers upstairs found out about the fire when a young woman ran across a dance floor with her hair blazing. Panic spread through the crowd, and people rushed toward the main exit, which was the only way in or out. But this was a revolving door, and it quickly became clogged with bodies. Hundreds of bodies were found piled against the Melody Lounge exit, on the stairs, and in front of the main revolving doors.

Heavy smoke and fumes from the burning palm trees poisoned other victims. Many died sitting at their tables in the dining room. A few people escaped by breaking windows in the basement, while others leaped from the roof. One group of young women were led into a walk-in refrigerator by a waiter and were later rescued, unharmed, by firefighters.

Although the fire department happened to be nearby because of another fire alarm, the Cocoanut Grove blaze spread so fast that there was nothing rescuers could do. In just 12 minutes, the entire building was destroyed, and fire roared through the roof.

Once the fire was finally put out, the grim task of removing bodies began. A total of 491 people were killed, and hundreds more were injured. Newly developed sulfa drugs were rushed to Boston from New York to treat burn victims.

The Cocoanut Grove disaster shocked the nation. Before the fire, nightclubs had been exempted from safety rules, but these laws were then extended to clubs as well. **Sprinkler systems** and plainly marked **exit doors** were now required. Doors had to open outward, and revolving doors had to be flanked by regular doors so that victims would not be trapped. If these laws had been in place in 1942, five hundred young lives would have been saved.

World War II was raging during the summer of 1944. But a crowd of six thousand people—mostly women and children—had their minds on happier events as they waited in the main tent of the **Ringling Bros. and Barnum & Bailey Circus** in Hartford, Connecticut. The show was about to begin!

The crowd didn't know it, but the circus tent was not made of fireproof canvas because that material was reserved for use in the war effort. Instead, the canvas had been treated with a makeshift mixture of **paraffin wax** and **gasoline**.

The crowd watched as the Flying Wallendas performed their high-wire act. An animal act had just finished, and trainers were guiding lions, tigers, leopards, and jaguars through a set of wire runways and into cages outside.

Just then, a small fire broke out on the canvas near the entrance, possibly from a carelessly dropped cigarette. Workers noticed the tiny blaze and began evacuating the tent. At first, the crowd left calmly but as flames spread through the tent at an alarming speed—fed quickly by the gasoline and paraffin—people began to run and push.

The band began to play "The Stars and Stripes Forever," which was a signal to circus workers that something was wrong. While several workers tried to put out the fire, panicked crowds stampeded to the exits, one of which was blocked by the animal runways. Then the fire roared up to the roof, completely consuming the canvas.

The Flying Wallendas managed to escape by crawling over the tops of the animal cages. They rushed back inside to rescue trapped victims, assisted by other circus performers, including the then famous clown, Emmett Kelly. Bandleader Merle Evans later said, "I have been through storms and blowdowns and circus wrecks, but never anything like this. I hope to God I never see a thing like this again."

Flaming pieces of canvas fell on spectators, setting hundreds of people on fire. Then the six support poles that held up the tent collapsed, crushing people underneath them. Once the tent fell, there was no way to escape. In less than ten minutes, 168 people—two-thirds of them children—were killed.

After the fire, five circus officials were arrested and charged with negligent manslaughter for not having enough firefighting equipment at the site. Six years later, in 1950, a former circus worker named Robert Segree confessed he had started the fire by deliberately placing a lit cigarette against the tent canvas. However, he later recanted his confession and was never tried.

July 6, 1944, became known as "the day the clowns cried." Ringling Bros. and Barnum & Bailey paid out more than $4 million to victims' families, most of which came directly out of the company's profits. The settlements were considered honest and fair, and everyone was paid without a court fight. The American government also allowed circuses to use fireproof canvas, despite the war effort, so that a tragedy like the Hartford circus fire would never happen again.

Few natural disasters are as terrifying as a **tsunami**. Most of these deadly tidal waves are caused by earthquakes beneath the ocean floor. Tsunamis can rush across the ocean for hundreds or even thousands of miles, building up into a giant wall of water that destroys everything in its path.

Residents living near **Hilo Bay** in the Hawaiian Islands didn't know they were in danger on the morning of April 1, 1946. But 2,500 miles away, an earthquake with a magnitude of 7.3 struck the **Aleutian Islands** near Alaska and started a tsunami that was racing across the ocean. Five hours after the earthquake, the wave reached Hilo Bay.

Before the tsunami struck, all the water flowed out of the bay. Many people, including large numbers of children who had been waiting for school buses, went down to the shore to see this unusual sight. They were caught unprepared when the water rushed back in with a wave more than twenty feet

high. Terrified residents tried to outrun the disaster, but most could not escape the wall of water. It swept over coconut trees and houses, destroying everything in its path. Some people clung to wreckage, while others were swept out to sea by the raging water.

Reporter Douglas Lovelace described the scene as he flew over Hilo: "Huge warehouses were flattened by the force of the water, and buildings had been crushed like eggshells and swept from their foundations... Railroad cars, automobiles, trucks, warehouses, molasses tanks, oil barges, and boats were strewn about like toothpicks. One oil barge has been tossed through a warehouse."

The **Red Cross** and the **U.S. Army** rushed to the area to help survivors. One of the most urgent needs was food, because most of the island's food supply had been stored in warehouses that were destroyed by the tsunami. Meanwhile, planes and ships searched the water for any survivors, in one of the greatest air–sea rescue operations in peacetime history.

The tsunami killed 164 people and destroyed 1,300 homes, leaving at least four thousand people homeless. It was the worst natural disaster ever to hit the Hawaiian Islands.

After this disaster, scientists created a tsunami warning system, which was put into operation in 1948 and is still used today. A warning is issued whenever a 6.75-magnitude earthquake strikes in or near the **Pacific Ocean**. Scientists monitor wave heights and issue a tsunami warning if they detect any unusual activity. In addition, many communities in Hawaii and coastal communities on the West Coast of the United States have sirens or other tsunami warning signals so residents can evacuate to higher ground.

When a ship loaded with flammable material catches fire in a crowded port city, the results can be devastating. Residents of **Texas City**, Texas, learned this lesson all too well on April 16, 1947.

Texas City was a thriving port on the Gulf of Mexico. A huge chemical plant surrounded by storage tanks for oil and gas sat near the water, and the harbor was often filled with ships carrying dangerous materials.

On April 16, the French freighter **SS *Grandcamp***

was in the harbor. The ship was loaded with fertilizer made of **nitrate** and **ammonia**. These materials are highly explosive and are used to make dynamite.

Early that morning, a fire broke out in a bag of fertilizer. The captain thought he could stop the fire by closing the hatch and turning on some steam jets to remove oxygen from the compartment and starve the fire. Unfortunately, the steam raised the temperature of the compartment to 350°F, which was hot enough for the ammonia and nitrate to explode.

Shortly after nine o'clock in the morning, as hundreds of spectators and firefighters stood on the docks, the *Grandcamp* blew up with a thunderous roar. Everyone on the ship and the nearby dock was killed instantly. The force was so destructive that the bodies were blown into tiny pieces. Windows were blown out miles away. Scientists in Denver, Colorado—over one thousand miles away—recorded the blast on equipment used to detect earthquakes.

The blast destroyed twenty blocks and knocked two small planes out of the sky. But things were about to get worse. Fire spread to the nearby **Monsanto** plant and its storage tanks. These also exploded, causing more fires and releasing dangerous chemical gases into the air. One reporter said he had seen such vast devastation only once before, after an atomic bomb destroyed Nagasaki, Japan, during World War II. Every electric line and all but one telephone line in the city was knocked down. An operator used the remaining phone line to call for help, saying, "For God's sake, send the Red Cross—thousands are dying!"

On April 17, a third explosion ripped through the area when a ship loaded with ammunition caught fire and blew up. This blast killed hundreds more people in an already devastated city.

Texas City burned for three days. Firefighters had no water to put out the fire because the explosions had damaged the city's water plant and pipes. By the time the fire was finally extinguished on April 18, a total of 752 people were dead, more than three thousand were injured, and one-third of the city was in ruins. Most of the bodies were so badly damaged that they could not be identified.

Financial estimates of the disaster were as high as $100 million. Most of the injured received monetary compensation from the federal government, and in just a few years, Texas City was completely rebuilt.

People attend sporting events for excitement and a good time. But sometimes sports can turn into deadly disasters, as spectators at one of the most famous auto races in the world found out on June 11, 1955.

The **Le Mans Grand Prix** is one of the most prestigious auto races in the world. This 24-hour endurance race is also one of the fastest. The course had originally been designed for slower speeds, and thus, did not have any warning lights to caution drivers. Before the race, French driver **Pierre Levegh** complained, "We need a signal system. Our cars go too fast." Sadly, Levegh would soon discover how true his words were.

During the thirty-second lap of the race, a Jaguar driver named **Mike Hawthorn** received a signal from his crew to pull off the track and into the pits to refill his car with gas. Hawthorn braked, and another car, driven by **Lance Macklin**, slowed and swerved to the left to avoid him. Macklin lost control of his car, which spun around and ended up across the track. Macklin managed to jump out of the car and run into the pits to safety.

Levegh saw Macklin's car in front of him, but since he was driving at 140 mph, he had no chance to stop. Instead, he gestured to the car behind him to stop, then tried to squeeze between Macklin's car and the wall. But there was no room.

Levegh's Mercedes-Benz 300 SLR hit Macklin's Austin-Healey, then struck an embankment beside the track. The Mercedes-Benz flipped end over end and disintegrated. The hood flew into the crowd, decapitating several spectators crowded close to the track. The engine and front axle somersaulted several hundred feet through the crowd, crushing many more in the stands. What was left of the car burst into flames as it sat on top of the embankment, sending blazing gasoline on the people below. In just a few seconds, eighty-two people were dead and seventy-six were seriously injured. One of the dead was Pierre Levegh, who had been thrown from his car and killed instantly.

The race went on, cars whizzing by the disaster as ambulances and fire trucks rushed to the scene. Spectators at the far end of the course had no idea anything terrible had happened until an announcement was made over the loudspeaker. Mike Hawthorn won the race, but as *Life* magazine reported, "Few spectators had the enthusiasm to cheer."

The French government temporarily suspended auto racing after the crash until an investigation could be held. The track at Le Mans was widened near the pits to allow drivers more room to get on and off, and the Grand Prix went on as scheduled the following year. But the crash is still remembered today as the worst disaster in auto-racing history and as one of the worst disasters ever to occur at a sporting event.

Before airplanes became a popular way to travel across the ocean, huge ships called luxury liners were the favored way to travel between North America and Europe. These ships were comfortable and elegant, but they were not immune to disaster.

The **SS *Andrea Doria*** was the finest ship in the **Italian Line** and the first liner built after World War II. The ship weighed almost 30,000 tons and had eleven decks. It was the first ocean liner to have three outdoor pools. Like other ships built after the war, the *Andrea Doria* also had a new safety feature called **radar** to alert the crew of other ships and obstacles in the water.

On July 17, 1956, the *Andrea Doria* left Genoa, Italy, to make its fifty-first trip across the Atlantic Ocean to New York. At nine o'clock on the evening of July 25, the ship began its approach to the Massachusetts coast. A thick fog surrounded the ship, so the captain ordered the ship to slow down.

Suddenly, the crew saw a green dot heading directly toward them on the radar screen. The dot represented **motor ship (MS) *Stockholm***, a Swedish liner that was heading to Europe. Although the *Stockholm* also had radar, the ship neither stopped nor slowed. The *Andrea Doria* blew its foghorn, but it was too late. At 11:45 p.m., the *Stockholm* plowed into the *Andrea Doria*, ripping a thirty-foot-long hole into its side and cutting the ship open from top to bottom. "It was just like an explosion," said one passenger on the *Andrea Doria*, "Like a very big firecracker."

As the *Andrea Doria*'s captain radioed for help, the ship began to fill with water and tilt toward the water. Passengers had to crawl on their hands and knees across the sharply tilting decks. The ship was listing so badly that it could not lower its lifeboats.

Fortunately, several other ships were in the area and quickly responded. Rescue efforts continued through the night, as passengers climbed on board other ships, including the *Stockholm*. Although that ship had been damaged, it was still afloat with a smashed bow "like a flattened tin bucket," according to news reports. By 4:30 a.m. the following morning, the *Andrea Doria* was empty. Just after 10:00 a.m., the queen vessel of the Italian Line sank to the bottom of the Atlantic Ocean.

Amazingly, only fifty-one people were killed in the collision, including forty-three people on board the *Andrea Doria* who were asleep in their cabins when the impact occurred. More than sixteen hundred passengers were safely rescued.

The captain of the *Andrea Doria* was so upset by the crash that he never sailed again. Meanwhile, the Italian Line and the **Swedish American Line** battled in court for months, each blaming the other for the crash. Finally, in January 1957, the companies settled out of court after an investigation ruled that both ships had been at fault.

Ships are not the only craft that travel across the world's oceans. Through the twentieth century, **submarines** became fairly common, patrolling beneath the surface. Unfortunately, when an accident occurs many miles underwater, there's little chance anyone can escape.

The **United States Ship (USS)** *Thresher* was the fastest and deepest-diving submarine when it was launched by the **United States Navy** in 1960. Its mission was to attack other submarines and ships. The *Thresher* was powered by **nuclear energy**, which meant it could stay underwater for weeks at a time. Nuclear-powered subs could even travel under the Arctic ice cap.

On April 10, 1963, there were 129 men aboard the *Thresher*. The sub was performing test dives in the Atlantic Ocean off the coast of New England, about 220 miles from Boston. Officials received a communication from the sub at 9:17 in the morning, but the ship did not radio in at its next scheduled time. There was only silence. The *Thresher* had simply disappeared.

At first, some people hoped that the sub had surfaced in rough seas and was simply having trouble communicating with its base. Then, about twelve hours later, the Navy reported seeing an oil slick in the Atlantic near where the *Thresher* had been operating. Oil slicks often form at the site of a wrecked submarine. Apparently, the sub had gone into a deep dive and never reemerged.

Although Navy officials scrambled to find the ship, they knew that there was little hope of locating survivors. The *Thresher* sank in 8,400 feet of water. At that depth, water pressure is so high that the submarine could not survive the force, and no reasonable rescue attempt could be made. All 129 sailors aboard the sub were presumed dead. It was the worst peacetime submarine disaster in the world.

As news of the disaster spread, many people worried that there could be a nuclear explosion or that the water would be contaminated by radioactive materials. However, the chief of naval operations said there was no chance of either scenario.

Although there was no hope of finding survivors, the Navy brought in special ships to search for the missing submarine. Several months after the *Thresher* disappeared, a craft called the *Trieste* found the remains of the submarine about eight thousand feet below sea level. Crew members took photographs of the wreckage. After the Navy studied these photos, they concluded that water had leaked into the engine room, causing the ship to flood and sink. As the sub sank deeper into the ocean, the water pressure became so powerful that it twisted the ship into an almost unrecognizable tangle of metal. No bodies were ever recovered from the wreckage, and the remains of the *Thresher* remain on the ocean floor to this day.

March 27, 1964, was Good Friday and the start of Easter weekend. As residents of **Anchorage**, Alaska's largest city, went about their business, they had no idea that the floor of the Prince William Sound had suddenly moved about ten miles upward, causing a tremendous **earthquake** that would devastate the city and most of the surrounding area.

At 5:36 p.m., the ground in Anchorage began to shake. The pavement rolled up and down like ocean waves and roads cracked and collapsed. Buildings crashed down, and houses slid off their foundations. The earthquake lasted four minutes, making it one of the longest quakes ever recorded. It was also one of the most powerful, measuring an astonishing 9.2 on the Richter scale.

The worst-hit part of the city was a neighborhood called Turnagain Bluff. Many of these homes had been built on soft ground that dissolved during the quake, sending houses sliding down the cliff.

Anne Thomas, who was eight years old at the time of the quake, ran out of the house with her mother and brother. She said she "heard glass smashing and the screech of our wooden house being pulled apart." After the trembling finally stopped, she looked back and said she saw "a huge black cliff... where our driveway had once been... I realized that our house had been up there, and during the earthquake we had slid with it all the way down to the shore of the inlet"—a drop of about three hundred feet.

The port city of **Seward** was also hit hard by the quake. The earthquake caused a huge landslide along the waterfront. Storage tanks, piers, and buildings slid into the water. Then the tanks exploded, setting fire to the area. Finally, a three-story tidal wave slammed into the city, washing ashore burning wreckage and oil through the streets. Most of the city was destroyed, but miraculously, only twelve people were killed.

The earthquake also created dangerous **tsunamis** along Alaska's coast and the American West Coast. Many homes on Kodiak Island and surrounding islands were destroyed by a giant wave that swept in from the bay. Four and half hours later, the tsunami drowned ten people in Crescent City, California, hundreds of miles away from Alaska. Four children in Oregon were also washed out to sea and drowned.

The Good Friday earthquake killed 130 people. Only nine were killed by the quake itself. The rest were drowned by the huge tidal waves that followed. After the disaster, Anchorage and the other damaged cities rebuilt, and many of the devastated waterfront areas were turned into parks. The earthquake also led to the creation of the **Alaska Tsunami Warning Center**, which alerts residents of Alaska, British Columbia, and the American West Coast about approaching tidal waves.

It was an ordinary day in the small mining village of **Aberfan**, Wales, United Kingdom. As they had countless times before, children sat in their classrooms of Pantglas Junior School. The school, along with a row of houses, was located in the shadow of an 800-foot-high pile of mining waste. This pile, called **slag**, included rocks, dirt, and pieces of coal.

For decades, Aberfan's residents had worried that the huge pile of slag might collapse. The pile sometimes moved slightly, but officials always assured the public that it was safe. At 9:30 a.m., the officials were proven to be egregiously incorrect, with tragic results.

A heavy rain, combined with an underground spring beneath the slag, caused the pile to suddenly give way. Two million tons of mud, rock, and coal hurtled toward the village in a flood a quarter-mile wide. One villager described hearing "the roar of the moving slag" and seeing "a black mass of waste pouring steadily on the school."

Most of the town's children were inside the school, but one boy was late. He witnessed the landslide as he hurried to school, and recalled, "...it looked like water pouring down the hillside... It hit the school like a big wave, spattering all over the place and crushing the building." The school was destroyed, along with fourteen nearby homes.

Hundreds of coal miners left their jobs and rushed to the disaster scene. They were joined by police and rescue personnel as they frantically dug through the wreckage,

hoping to find survivors. Some men used shovels, while others dug with their bare hands. Parents heard the news and rushed to the site where the school had been.

The death toll was tremendous, especially for such a small community. Of the 144 victims, 116 were children attending the Pantglas Junior School. The death toll represented half of all the children in the village, and almost all the town's children between the ages of nine and eleven. Many of the victims had suffocated in the mud, while others had been killed by the collapsing buildings.

Angry parents demanded that their children's death certificates read "Buried alive by the National Coal Board." One man, who lost his daughter in the landslide, told reporters: "There have been reports about the slag heap moving for the past ten years. The thing is built on a bog. It should never had been put up there. I don't want to live here anymore."

An investigation by the government of Wales sided with the parents. It found that a buildup of water under the slag heap had created a "water bomb" that burst and turned the slag into a deadly **landslide**. Wales blamed the **National Coal Board** for the disaster because it had not inspected the slag heap for four years. Despite these findings, there were no criminal proceedings against the coal board, although a disaster fund raised more than £17 million to help the families and remove other slag heaps from the area.

Florence is one of the most beautiful cities in the world. Part of its beauty comes from the **Arno** river, which flows through the city. However, this river can also create tremendous destruction and ugliness.

Historians have recorded major floods of the Arno since 1177. In 1545, Leonardo da Vinci drew up plans for a series of dams and locks to prevent flooding, but they were never built.

October 1966 had been a very wet month. Then on November 3–4, nineteen inches of rain fell on the city. This was more than the area usually received in four months' time. To make matters worse, the operators of a dam above Florence neglected to release the excess water during October. By the time they did open the floodgates, an enormous wall of water flowed out—straight into Florence.

In just two hours on the night of November 4, the Arno water level rose eighteen feet. A man standing on the historic **Ponte Vecchio** bridge recalled seeing the water rush past at 40 mph, carrying trees and pieces of debris in its wake. Four hours later, the Ponte Vecchio was underwater, along with most of the city's streets.

As the water flooded the city, Florence's sewer system backed up, sending human waste through the streets. Many residents who lived in lower-floor apartments drowned, while those on the upper floors were trapped by the rising waters until they could be rescued by helicopters.

When the rain finally stopped on November 6, Florence's residents began tallying the grim toll of the disaster. The flood left 144 people dead and 5,000 homeless, and it destroyed 6,000 businesses.

Florence had been home to the largest collection of Renaissance artwork, but these items also fell victim to the raging water. Torrents filled museums, churches, and historic sites, covering paintings, sculptures, and religious artifacts with fifteen to twenty feet of water and mud. One million historic books in the city's **Biblioteca Nazionale Centrale** became waterlogged. Priceless telescopes used by Galileo were saved because the director of the museum that housed them carried the instruments out as she escaped along a window ledge.

Volunteers from all over the world came to Florence to help the city and restore the artwork. They took the waterlogged books from the library and placed them in special drying equipment. Other volunteers washed statues and dug out precious treasures from the mud. Residents soon began calling them **"mud angels."**

After the flood, Florence slowly began to plan and build more dams that were sophisticated enough to protect the city from future flooding.

When weather forecasters first noticed a tropical depression forming off the western coast of Africa in August 1969, they had no idea that the storm would become one of the most destructive ever to hit the United States. By the time **Hurricane Camille** was done with the American South, it would go down in history as a merciless killer.

Weather forecasters watched Camille as it traveled across the Atlantic Ocean. By August 14, it was in the Caribbean, about 480 miles south of Miami. Two days later, the storm slammed into Mississippi and Louisiana. More than two hundred thousand people fled their homes along the Gulf of Mexico, seeking shelter on higher ground.

The worst of the storm hit just west of Gulfport, Mississippi. Winds up to 190 mph battered the city. "The wind is blowing rocks," said a Gulfport police officer. "There's a boat out in the parking lot here and we're three blocks from the harbor."

Camille also sent a 20- to 25-foot-high storm surge of water rushing through the area. Beach houses were swept into the ocean. One group of twelve people defied evacuation orders and had a hurricane party at the Richelieu Apartments on the Gulf Coast; every partygoer was killed when the storm collapsed the structure. A few blocks away, a motel was destroyed when waves carried several ships into the building.

By two o'clock in the morning, Camille had moved out of the area. Rescuers, including members of the armed forces, went in on special boats to rescue survivors. They found natural gas lines ruptured, water and food contaminated, and dead bodies floating in between debris from wrecked houses. To make matters worse, hundreds of poisonous cottonmouth snakes had crawled into Gulfport from nearby swamps, trying to escape the rising water.

Camille was not finished with the United States yet. Although meteorologists expected the storm to die out as it moved over land, Camille still had significant amounts of moisture in its storm clouds. On August 19, a total of thirty-one inches of rain fell over Nelson County, Virginia. Scientists estimated that four hundred million gallons of water fell on the area in just four hours, an event that only occurs once every thousand years. The rain caused flooding and mudslides that killed almost two hundred people.

The head of the **National Hurricane Center** in Miami described Hurricane Camille as "the greatest recorded storm ever to hit a heavily populated area of the Western Hemisphere." Camille killed at least three hundred people. However, the death toll would have been much higher if science had not developed ways to forecast storms. Because meteorologists tracked Camille from the time the storm began, thousands of people had a chance to evacuate their homes and escape disaster.

In some parts of the world, storms and other natural disasters can kill hundreds of thousands. These staggering death tolls often occur because of crowded conditions and poor housing construction. This was the case for one of the deadliest disasters to ever strike **East Pakistan** (now **Bangladesh**) in 1970.

Much of East Pakistan was made of low-lying islands and coastal areas. Even though this area is prone to ferocious storms, called **cyclones** that form over the **Bay of Bengal**, hundreds of thousands of people make their homes there. Even today, the area is so densely populated that there few other places for residents to live.

Even though residents of East Pakistan had been accustomed to storms, the events of November 12 took them by surprise. Only three weeks earlier, residents had evacuated the area when they heard that a smaller storm was on the way. The storm did not do much damage, so when an American weather satellite sent information about a new storm approaching the area on November 11, the government ignored the calls and did not inform residents of the danger.

The cyclone struck in the middle of the night on November 12. Most residents were sleeping in flimsy straw houses that could never have withstood the wind and rain. When a 50-foot-high tidal wave swept over land that was only twenty feet above sea level, it washed sleeping residents out to sea. Then 150-mile-per-hour winds destroyed everything in their path, including hospitals, power lines, and roads. The area was cut off, and the rest of the world did not even know about the tragedy until two days later.

When rescue crews finally arrived in East Pakistan, they were met with an unimaginable disaster. Entire towns had been destroyed, and hundreds of thousands of people were missing or dead. On one island alone, twenty thousand people had been washed out to sea. Rescuers reported that many bodies were washing up on shore, and survivors were pushing them back out to sea with bamboo poles. So many people had died that one newspaper reported it was easier to count the living than the dead.

Even after the storm passed, the death toll continued to rise because the dead bodies created a breeding ground for disease. Water and food supplies were contaminated, and many people who had survived the storm died of cholera or typhoid. One journalist reported there were so many decaying bodies that "even from an airplane, it was possible to smell death."

Countries around the world rushed to East Pakistan's aid. Relief workers and doctors arrived from all over Europe and Asia, and engineers came from the United States and Great Britain to rebuild transportation and communications systems. The **International Red Cross** was on hand to distribute medicine, food, and water. Slowly, life in East Pakistan returned to normal.

The storm's final death toll was approximately three hundred thousand people. It was the worst tropical cyclone of the twentieth century, and one of the worst natural disasters ever to strike our world.

Residents of **Nicaragua** received a very unwelcome Christmas present just a few days before the holiday. While they were sleeping, a series of powerful earthquakes struck right under the capital city of **Managua**. The city, home to one-fifth of Nicaragua's population, was turned into a death chamber.

The earthquakes, which measured up to 6.2 on the Richter scale, caused 75 percent of Managua's buildings to collapse. After the quakes, damaged structures continued to fall. Some were so fragile that even the vibrations of a passing truck could cause them to collapse. The U.S. Army sent demolition experts to Managua to destroy dangerous structures, including the U.S. Embassy.

The city was also consumed by fire when severed gas lines exploded. "It didn't take long until terrible fires lit the whole town," said survivor Ricardo Gomez. "Soon, the gasoline blasts started, and the sky was lit up as if by fireworks."

Army personnel, Red Cross workers, and volunteers from around the world poured into Managua to help. They were appalled at the devastation. "This is a city that was but is no more," said Lieutenant Colonel Jose Alagret, the commander of the **Army Corps of Engineers**.

Life for survivors was extremely difficult. The city was overrun with looters who stole food and other supplies from markets and warehouses. Nicaragua's government sent in their army with orders to shoot looters on sight, but the soldiers could do little to control the destruction.

Officials also worried that disease would spread rapidly because of the decaying bodies buried under the rubble. To encourage people to leave the city, the government cut off food supplies and forced the Red Cross to shut down their emergency food stations. In response, the Red Cross set up aid centers outside the city to help those fleeing from the devastation.

The earthquake claimed between four and six thousand lives, injured twenty thousand, and left two hundred fifty thousand people homeless. One additional fatality created a sad footnote to the disaster. Famous baseball star Roberto Clemente, a native of Puerto Rico, had collected supplies and medicine for the survivors, and he chartered several stocked planes from Puerto Rico to Nicaragua. However, on New Year's Eve, Clemente left Puerto Rico on one of the planes, intending to distribute the supplies himself, and the plane crashed, killing everyone on board.

The Managua earthquake was caused by a **fault line** that ran directly underneath the city. Earthquakes had occurred there before, including one in 1931 that killed one thousand people. Although the 1972 quake devastated the city, it caused very little damage to surrounding areas, and scientists recommended that Managua be rebuilt in a different location to avoid future disasters. However, the city was rebuilt at the same location, which means the likelihood of another terrible quake remains high.

River canyons can be wonderful places to hike and camp. But a sudden rainstorm can change a quiet mountain stream into a raging wall of water with no escape.

Big Thompson Canyon is a popular tourist spot in the Rocky Mountains of Colorado. Most of the 25-mile-long gorge is so narrow that there is barely room for a highway and the river, which is little more than an 18-inch-deep stream. Wider spots in the canyon feature cabins, motels, and campgrounds for the thousands of tourists who visit each summer.

On July 31, 1976, about three thousand visitors and residents were in the canyon. Although the weather was dry, thunderstorms were raging in the mountains near the head of the canyon. Almost twelve inches of rain fell between 6:30 p.m. and 10:30 p.m. that night—more than the average yearly rainfall for the area. "Raindrops a half-inch in diameter were coming straight down," reported one state trooper. "My slicker pockets filled with water almost immediately."

The torrential rains turned the shallow stream into a raging river nineteen feet high and traveling more than twenty feet per second. Around 8:00 p.m. that night, police received reports that part of the highway had washed out. They began evacuating people from the canyon, but since the river was still calm, and it was not raining in the lower parts of the canyon, many people refused to leave. By the time they understood the danger, it was too late.

"Campers were being washed away, and big propane tanks were coming downstream, spinning like crazy, starting to explode," recalled one survivor. Another, who lived in a town in the canyon, explained: "You've got to realize that by the time the flood hit us, it wasn't just water. There was a lot of solid material—dirt, rocks, buildings, cars, and concrete—that was carried along with us."

People camping in the narrow canyon realized the only way out was up. They climbed up the sides as fast as they could, then hung on to the rocks as the water thundered by below them and rain pounded down from above. "You could barely see anything," one survivor recalled. "You could hear the loud roar of the water and all the noise—all the trees breaking, the banging of the automobiles, the people screaming and hollering and crying."

Three hours after it started, the flood was over. Helicopters and Jeeps went into the canyon to rescue thousands of stranded people. The helicopters also picked up the bodies of 139 people, including two police officers, who had died. Many of the bodies were trapped inside cars or buried in several feet of mud.

The Big Thompson Canyon flood was the deadliest natural disaster in Colorado's history. Over the next few years, improvements in weather forecasting equipment helped reduce the chances of so many people becoming trapped in another disaster. However, the combination of narrow canyons and heavy rain will continue to cause devastating flash floods.

Planes do not necessarily have to be in the air to cause a catastrophic crash. Indeed, the deadliest accidental **plane crash** in history occurred on the runway, when human error caused a terrible mix-up that led to disaster.

This terrible accident occurred at a small airport in Tenerife, part of the Canary Islands off the coast of northern Africa. The small airport wasn't usually used for jet traffic, but the islands' larger airport had been closed because a group of terrorists had set off a bomb there. That was why two Boeing 747s, a **KLM** jet from the Netherlands and a **Pan American World Airways (Pan Am)** jet from New York, were sitting on the runway on March 27, 1977.

At 4:40 p.m. in the afternoon, the KLM jet was cleared for takeoff. The Pan Am jet was instructed to wait in a small area at the end of the runway. The KLM jet would taxi down the runway, turn around, then take off. After it had cleared the runway, the Pan Am jet would follow.

A thick **fog** descended on the airport just before the planes were scheduled to take off. Another problem was that the Dutch crew of the KLM plane had trouble understanding the Spanish-accented English of the control tower personnel, and they also had interference on the radio frequency. Somehow, the KLM plane misunderstood its instructions and began taxiing down the runway too early.

The Pan Am pilot was shocked to see the KLM jet zooming toward him. "What's he doing? He'll kill us all!" the pilot shouted as he tried to drive his plane off the runway and into a field. But it was too late. The KLM jet plowed into the Pan Am plane, ripping completely through it. Both planes exploded in a fiery roar.

The crash and fire were so intense that everyone on the KLM plane was killed. Most of the passengers on the Pan Am jet also died. However, the Pan Am pilot had managed to steer the jet partly off the runway, saving the lives of his crew and the passengers seated in the front of the plane. "Most of the people sitting in the first six seats made it," one survivor reported.

The fire was so intense that some of the bodies were burned beyond recognition, and only metal fragments remained of the two planes. Rescue workers moved the hundreds of bodies into the airplane hangar and laid them out in two rows, one for each plane. A reporter described the scene as: "More bodies, more parts of bodies than anyone could stand to count, more bodies than the eye could take in with a single glance, more bodies contorted, bent, and blackened than a dozen nightmares could conjure up."

A total of 570 people were killed: 249 on the KLM plane and 321 on the Pan Am plane. There were just seventy-two survivors, all of whom owed their lives to the quick thinking of the Pan Am pilot.

Strange things can happen when the lights go out. A **blackout** that plunged **New York City** into darkness on the hot, stormy night of July 13, 1977, brought out the worst in many people.

New York City had gone through blackouts before. On November 9, 1965, a massive blackout knocked out power to thirty million people in the American Northeast. Although they

were frightened and inconvenienced, New Yorkers remained calm. They helped each other by directing traffic, sharing candles and flashlights, and getting to know strangers who were trapped with them in subway cars and elevators. The event became known as "the night the lights went out," and it was fondly remembered by many who experienced it.

The 1977 blackout, however, was very different. That blackout occurred in the middle of a hot, tense summer. New York City was in financial trouble. There was a lot of anger and unrest in poor, disadvantaged communities over cutbacks in city services. The crime rate was high, and many New Yorkers were terrified by a serial killer nicknamed the "Son of Sam."

On July 13, four lightning strikes knocked out power lines feeding the city. Although other areas did not lose power, New York City was in total darkness by 9:40 p.m. Without air conditioning to cool their apartments, people poured out into the streets in search of some relief. In some neighborhoods, the mood was festive and friendly. But in others, things quickly became violent.

Looters rampaged through stores, carrying out furniture, televisions, clothes, and other consumer goods. Fifty cars were stolen from a dealership in the Bronx. New York City police made more than thirty-seven hundred arrests, but they were helpless to stop thousands of people from smashing store windows and stealing merchandise.

The looters were not necessarily angry. They simply used the blackout as an opportunity to let off some steam and engage in activity they usually would not have done. The mob mentality also encouraged people to commit crimes that otherwise would have been unthinkable.

Other troublemakers set fires. The fire department responded to more than a thousand fires that night—six times the average rate.

It took twenty-five hours for power to be restored to all of New York City. City officials, including **Mayor Abraham Beame**, were furious at **Con Edison**, New York City's power authority. Con Edison claimed that the blackout was a result of natural events, but residents and officials could not understand how a few lightning bolts could knock out power to millions of people. The city claimed that Con Edison was guilty of "at the very least gross negligence—and at the worst something far more serious." Businesses that suffered financial damages because of the blackout successfully sued Con Edison to recover their losses.

After the power came back on, store owners cleaned up the mess. The anger subsided, and soon life was back to normal. But no one would ever forget what had happened—and what might happen again—on the night that the lights went out.

Many people believe **nuclear power** is a safe, clean, cheap way to produce energy. Others are convinced the dangers that come with nuclear power outweigh its benefits. The United States had its first brush with nuclear disaster in late March 1979 at the **Three Mile Island power station** in Pennsylvania.

At 3:48 a.m. on the morning of March 28, just three months after the plant opened, several pumps in Unit Two broke down. Without the pumps to circulate water through the reactor, the temperature inside soared, melting rods filled with radioactive uranium.

As alarms sounded through the control room, an operator opened a valve to release water from the reactor and send it into a waste tank. But the highly pressurized water burst the pipes and flooded the reactor, where it quickly turned into a cloud of radioactive steam. This steam flowed up a vent stack and barreled out into the open air.

At seven o'clock in the morning, state authorities were informed that a disaster was underway at Three Mile Island. Partly due to ignorance—and partly due to their desire to avoid panic—officials downplayed what was going on. In reality, the situation was getting worse.

The high temperature inside the reactor caused water to break down into oxygen and hydrogen molecules. The hydrogen formed a huge bubble. If the bubble became large enough, the reactor could suffer a meltdown and release huge amounts of radiation into the atmosphere.

On Friday morning, Pennsylvania's governor asked all children and pregnant women within five miles of the plant to leave the area. Children were pulled out of schools and taken on sealed school buses to other schools ten to fifteen miles away. Although some residents had already left the area, the evacuation of the children stirred up a panic. More than fifty thousand people flooded out of the towns around the plant.

On Saturday, operators managed to reduce the size of the hydrogen bubble and eventually break it up. The **Nuclear Regulatory Commission** declared the emergency over on Monday, April 9. Everyone was encouraged to return home.

However, many questions remained unanswered. No one knew if the radiation in the air and the soil would make people sick. Scientists and doctors performed many studies of living things around Three Mile Island. Some found evidence of plant mutations and increased cancers in animals, while other studies said there was no sign of increased cancers in humans.

Meanwhile, the Nuclear Regulatory Commission issued a report on the disaster. It blamed a combination of human error, poor equipment, and design flaws for the accident, saying the operators had "inadvertently turned a minor accident into a major one because they could not tell what was really happening inside the reactor."

The Three Mile Island accident led to increased protests against nuclear power. Several nuclear power plants in planning were never built because of the mounting public pressure, and safety and training programs were improved at other plants. Despite these efforts, the danger of another nuclear disaster in the United States is still all too real.

It was the beginning of the Memorial Day weekend, and Chicago's O'Hare International Airport was filled with travelers. No one boarding **American Airlines Flight 191** to Los Angeles had any idea that carelessness was about to lead to the deadliest aviation accident in American history.

The **McDonnell Douglass DC-10** jet was loaded with 273 passengers when it took off at three o'clock in the afternoon on May 25. But the plane had only reached an altitude of four hundred feet when something went terribly wrong. As onlookers watched in horror, the left engine fell off the plane.

A man landing on another plane as Flight 191 took off recalled, "The young fellow in front of me said, 'Look at that.' I looked over and he said, 'The engine fell off.' We watched the plane as far as we could. The plane went on a fairly level course and gained just a little teeny bit of altitude and then it nosed off to the left, the wing went down, and it was just one solid mass of flames all at once."

The plane rolled over and plunged to the ground. Instantly, a tremendous explosion rocked the area as the jet fuel exploded. "As it impacted, flames shot out to where I thought my face was going to be singed," said a man driving past the crash on a nearby highway. "When I looked back, it looked like an atomic bomb explosion."

All 273 passengers and crew on the plane were killed instantly in the crash and explosion. The fire was so hot that it was several hours before anyone could get close enough to the wreckage to remove the bodies. Flames and smoke could be seen in downtown Chicago ten miles away.

A federal judge immediately ordered all 275 DC-10s in service to stop flying "in the interest of public safety." Investigators studied the crash and finally determined that a three-inch-long bolt holding the engine on the plane had broken, causing it to fall off. The broken bolt also damaged the hydraulic lines that controlled the wings. Although a plane can fly with the loss of one engine, the loss of the hydraulics made it impossible for the pilot to keep the plane in the air.

Further investigation revealed that American Airlines mechanics had not removed the engines correctly during maintenance procedures. Instead of removing the engine and the bolt separately, as the manufacturer had recommended, the mechanics removed everything at once with a forklift. This action had cracked the bolt. This revelation meant that every American Airlines DC-10 plane would be too dangerous to fly. Immediately, all DC-10s around the world were checked and repaired if necessary. Once all were inspected and found to be safe, the DC-10s returned to the sky. The disaster was a terrible price to pay for safety.

Hurricanes can cover a large area and last for more than a week. **Hurricane David** was one of the deadliest storms to strike the Caribbean and the East Coast of the United States, leaving a trail of destruction from the island of **Dominica** all the way up to **New England**.

Hurricane David first showed its strength in the Caribbean. It struck the small island of Dominica on August 31, where its high winds and heavy rains killed twenty-two people. But that was just the beginning of David's fury.

The storm moved on to Puerto Rico and then the Dominican Republic. This nation was the hardest hit as 150-mile-per-hour winds and high tides killed more than one thousand people, left one hundred fifty thousand homeless, and destroyed 90 percent of the nation's crops. Houses, cars, and hotels were smashed to pieces, palm trees and utility poles were ripped out of the ground, and roads and sidewalks were twisted and smashed. Waves washed right into the lobbies of hotels along the beach. In the town of Padre las Casas, four hundred people were killed when flood waters from a river roared through the church and school where they had gone for shelter. A few people survived by climbing onto the church steeple.

By September 3, David was on its way to Florida. Residents of Palm Beach braced themselves as the storm hit them with 90-mile-per-hour winds. Trailers and homes were smashed, and a condominium complex had its back wall peeled off by a tornado caused by the storm. "I've never seen so much destruction in one place," said a local police chief. Fortunately, since most residents had evacuated, only five deaths were reported, including a man who was electrocuted when the mast of his sailboat hit a power line as he was towing the boat out of the water. Several other victims suffered heart attacks or died in traffic accidents caused by the storm.

The storm moved up the coast and struck Georgia, South Carolina, and North Carolina. The area received up to nine inches of rain, and waves flooded streets and houses. A large oak tree in Savannah, Georgia, was split in half when a lamp post fell on it.

Although the hurricane weakened as it moved up the coast, it was still a powerful storm as it reached New Jersey, New York, and Connecticut. Several people drowned, including a police officer and two boys who were sucked into a storm drain in New Jersey. The storm also knocked out power to hundreds of thousands of people in the Northeast before finally fading away over Newfoundland, Canada.

Although the death toll in the United States was relatively small, Hurricane David killed more than one thousand people in the Dominican Republic. The storm's total death toll was more than eleven hundred people, and it caused more than $1.2 billion in damages, making it one of the worst Atlantic hurricanes ever.

◆ Take several thousand fans eager to see their favorite band, general admission seating, and poor crowd control, and the results can be tragic. That was the lesson learned by the people of Cincinnati, Ohio, and the rock group **The Who**.

The Who were on a sold-out concert tour of the United States in 1979. On December 3, the band played at **Riverfront Coliseum** in Cincinnati. Like most concerts at the Coliseum, the event had "festival seating." The first people to enter the auditorium rushed to the best seats or simply stood in front of the stage.

Thousands of The Who fans gathered outside the Coliseum several hours before the concert began at 8:00 p.m. Security guards made no effort to communicate with the crowd or organize them into lines. Finally, a few doors opened, and the crowd surged forward, pushing to get into the narrow doorways. Then, inexplicably, those entrances were shut, and different doors opened. There were never enough open doors to admit the thousands of fans, and the scene soon became a terrifying **crush** of people.

The movement of the crowd forced people off their feet, and the pressing of bodies made it hard to breathe. A young man in the crowd recalled, "I remember that I had to time my breathing so that I would take in air during the waves when the pressure let up long enough to expand the lungs."

Another fan described how people were being trampled underfoot. "I felt my leg being pulled to the right. The crowd shifted again, and I reached down and grabbed an arm at my leg. I struggled for a while and finally pulled up a young girl who also had a young boy clinging to her limbs. They were barely conscious, and their faces were filled with tears."

Finally, enough doors were opened to ease the crush. Fans entered the lobby and saw bodies lying everywhere, along with hundreds of pairs of shoes that had been ripped off victims in the crush.

Strangely enough, most of the fans at the concert had entered through a different set of doors and had no idea that a disaster had occurred. The Who also was not told of the tragedy until after they concluded their show. "I went on inside and was stunned to find the place practically full," said a fan who had endured the crush. "I settled in and tried to enjoy the concert, still trying to convince myself that no one had really *died*." But eleven young people *had* died and dozens more were injured.

The disaster set off a storm of controversy and investigations into problems with crowd control. Cincinnati established a committee to review safety precautions at the Coliseum and other arenas, and the group eventually issued a ninety-page document with more than one hundred recommendations. Cincinnati, along with several other cities, banned festival seating. However, the sad truth is that fans are still seriously injured or killed at concerts and sporting events today.

THE CINCINNATI ENQUIRER
Stampede Kills 11 Persons At Coliseum Rock Concert

Tuesday
Dec. 4, 1979

People expect to be safe in their homes, schools, and communities. Unfortunately, environmental pollution can create hazardous conditions that destroy entire regions.

Residents of **Love Canal**, a neighborhood in **Niagara Falls, New York**, had no idea that, between 1946 and 1953, the **Hooker Chemicals and Plastics Corporation** had dumped more than 42 million pounds of pesticides and other poisonous chemicals into the canal that gave the community its name. Some of these toxic chemicals were known to cause cancer and other serious diseases.

In 1953, the local school board bought sixteen acres of land from Hooker Chemical and built a new school there. Soon, students started suffering from serious disorders, such as seizures, blood diseases, kidney failure, and cancer. Families in the community also reported severe medical problems. Many women suffered miscarriages or gave birth to children with birth defects or disabilities.

Residents also wondered why black sludge sometimes oozed into their yards and why their basements smelled so bad. Trees and other plants died. Pets and children suffered burns and rashes after playing in the fields around the old dumpsite.

Finally, during the 1970s, families in Love Canal organized and began to ask for answers. They spoke to local, state, and federal officials. Newspapers wrote stories about their efforts. It did not take long for residents to learn that their community was built on a **toxic waste dump**. People were terrified for their health and the health of their children. They wanted to move away, but they could not afford to leave without selling their homes. And no one wanted to buy a home that was contaminated with deadly chemicals.

On August 2, 1978, the New York State Health Commissioner reported that "Love Canal is a great and imminent peril to the health of the general public." Two days later, residents formed the Love Canal Homeowners Association to pressure the government to pay for them to relocate. It took more than a year, but on August 5, 1979, **President Jimmy Carter** declared Love Canal a disaster area and authorized the federal government to pay $20 million to buy homes and relocate 239 families. Nine months later, after pressure from the Association, a second emergency was declared so the rest of the Love Canal families could move away.

Love Canal led to the passage of the **Comprehensive Environmental Response Compensation and Liability Act (CERCLA) of 1980**, more commonly known as the **"Superfund" law**. This act set up a multibillion-dollar fund to clean up toxic waste dumps. In 1986, Congress passed another law to assist communities hit by **environmental disasters**.

Specially trained workers spent several years cleaning up Love Canal. They capped the dumpsite with a layer of clay and pumped out contaminated water. In 1988, some areas of Love Canal were declared safe. Houses there were sold at below-market value and were quickly purchased. However, most former residents—many of whom had lost children and other family members to cancer and other diseases—refused to return. For them, Love Canal would always be a disaster that had ruined their lives.

Many people think **volcanic eruptions** only occur on faraway tropical islands, but the continental United States was the scene of one violent eruption in 1980.

Mount St. Helens is located in southern Washington state. It is part of the **Cascade Range**, which stretches from northern California up to British Columbia, Canada. The mountain had been quiet for 123 years, but things began to change during March 1980. Minor

earthquakes shook the area, and the volcano let off plumes of steam and ash. Scientists rushed to the area to study this suddenly active volcano. Meanwhile, state police forced most residents to evacuate the area.

At 8:32 a.m. on the morning of May 18, a tremendous landslide and earthquake ripped away one side of the volcano, releasing a cloud of ash and hot gas. Traveling up to 330 mph, the blast cloud destroyed everything within 150 square miles. A few seconds later, another explosion sent a cloud of ash and gas sixteen miles into the sky.

The eruption reduced the volcano's height from 9,677 feet to 8,367 feet and created a half-mile-diameter crater at the top of the mountain. Spirit Lake, which had been located at the base of the mountain, had vanished under five hundred feet of debris. The meadows, streams, and forests that had surrounded the mountain were obliterated by tons of mud and rocks from the largest recorded avalanche in history.

So much ash was released from the volcano that it darkened the sky for almost two hundred miles. Towns in Washington, Montana, and Idaho recorded ash falling from the sky like snow, and snowplows were sent out to remove up to a foot of ash from the streets.

Rescue crews rushed into the area. Although about two thousand people had been evacuated from the area before the eruption, many scientists and some residents were still near the volcano. Crews reported finding bodies all over the devastated area. An Air Force captain found two dead bodies in a car fifteen miles west of the volcano. "These people were fried with the heat," he reported. "Trees and all the vegetation was laid out flat—singed, burned, steaming, sizzling—a terrible looking thing."

In all, fifty-seven people were killed in the eruption and landslide, along with five thousand deer, fifteen hundred elk, two hundred black bears, and thousands of birds and smaller animals. It was the worst volcanic disaster in American history.

After the eruption, Mount St. Helens and the surrounding area were renamed the **Mount St. Helens National Volcanic Monument**. The region became a center for scientists studying volcanic eruptions. Other researchers documented the changes in the region around the mountain. Although this area was barren and lifeless after the eruption, in time, flowers, grass, and even trees began to grow again. As the vegetation grew thicker, various animal species also returned to the area. Today, Mount St. Helens is one of the most unusual national parks in the United States.

People flock to **Las Vegas** every year to have a good time in the city's casinos, showrooms, and theaters. The city is filled with luxury high-rise hotels to house the huge numbers of tourists who come to Las Vegas every year. On November 21, 1980, one of these hotels and fun palaces became a deathtrap.

The **MGM Grand Hotel and Casino** (now Bally's Las Vegas) was built in 1973. The build-

ing was twenty-six stories tall and covered approximately two million square feet. The casino and showroom on the ground floor covered an area larger than a football field.

About 7:00 a.m. on the morning of Friday, November 21, a fire started behind a wall socket in The Deli, a restaurant near the casinos on the ground floor of the hotel. The cause of the fire was two uninsulated wires from a refrigerator rubbing together as the unit vibrated. "It took a long time for the fault to generate enough heat to make a fire," said Deputy Chief Ralph King of the Clark County Fire Department. "There was a time factor of approximately six years—this didn't just happen overnight."

The fire spread quickly into the casino area, where it became an inferno. The casino had no sprinkler system, and it was filled with flammable furniture, wall coverings, and plastic pipes and fixtures. Then, the fire spread into the building's air return system and ductwork, sending deadly smoke and heat into the upper floors of the hotel.

About five thousand guests and staff were in the hotel at the time of the fire.

Most were sleeping in their rooms and became trapped. Some broke windows or hung from balconies, waving towels and bedsheets in an effort to attract rescuers' attention. Others fled down the stairwells or were plucked from the roof by helicopters.

Unfortunately, many people tried to use the elevators to escape. This turned out to be a fatal mistake because the fire had shut down the elevator system. Firefighters found many bodies inside the elevators. "There were piles of bodies around the elevator doors," recalled one firefighter. "The worst thing I remember about it was a father with his arms around his family. If they had gone to the stairwell, they would have been fine."

In all, eighty-five people were killed in the MGM Grand fire, and another six hundred fifty were injured. The fire led to many changes in building codes to make high-rises safer. More sprinklers were used, and flammable materials such as plastics were banned. In addition, modern elevators are now programmed to lock and return to the bottom floor during an emergency, preventing people from finding themselves trapped inside.

The MGM Grand Hotel and Casino was rebuilt to include these new safety features. "I don't think I'll ever see an MGM fire again because our life safety systems are so outstanding," said Deputy Chief King. Like so many other disasters, the tragic lessons of the MGM Grand fire saved many lives in the future.

In 1980, doctors and researchers noticed a mysterious new disease that was spreading quickly, especially among sexually active men identifying as gay. Strong, young, and healthy men became weak, emaciated, and sick because their immune systems could not fight off the rare illness. Within a few years, the victims were dead.

Researchers called this new illness **acquired immunodeficiency syndrome (AIDS)**. AIDS was caused by the **human immunodeficiency virus (HIV)**, and it was spread through bodily fluids like blood. Risk of contracting the virus was higher for people who engaged in unprotected sex or who had multiple sexual partners as well as people with substance use disorders who shared needles. Because the disease was spread through blood, people who received blood transfusions were also at risk.

AIDS quickly became an **epidemic** in the gay community. At first, there was little sympathy for the victims. Many conservative politicians and religious leaders even said AIDS victims deserved to die. Children and teenagers who had contracted AIDS through blood transfusions were denied admission to schools, and their families were often chased out of their homes by violence and threats. Victims faced prejudice and discrimination as rumors spread that people could catch AIDS just by touching someone who had the disease.

The public began to realize that AIDS could affect anybody after several celebrities, including movie star **Rock Hudson** and basketball player **Magic Johnson**, admitted that they had the disease. Stories of victims such as **Ryan White**, a teenage hemophiliac, also captured the public's attention and sympathy.

AIDS quickly became a political flash point. Patients and their families and friends organized into advocacy groups such as **AIDS Coalition to Unleash Power (ACT-UP)** to demand equal access to medical care for all patients, regardless of economic status or sexual orientation.

Meanwhile, medical science struggled to develop a cure. Over the years, AIDS patients have been treated with many different drugs, which have slowed the progression of the disease. More recently, drugs have been developed that can help prevent contraction of HIV both before and after exposure. AIDS is now seen as a long-term, chronic illness rather than an immediate death sentence. Someday, scientists hope to find a vaccine that will cure the world of the disease.

AIDS is truly a worldwide pandemic. Although the rate of infection and death has stabilized in the United States and Western Europe, it has exploded in other parts of the world. Southern African nations have been especially hard-hit. In Zimbabwe, one in four adults has been infected with HIV. India, China, Indonesia, and Eastern Europe have also reported huge increases in the disease. In the United States, 34,800 new HIV infections occurred in 2019. Since 1980, more than thirty-six million people have died of AIDS. Although much progress has been made against this disease, it will continue to be a disaster for millions of victims around the world.

The simplest things can cause disasters. In **Mansi, India**, a cow crossing the railroad tracks may have killed more than five hundred people in the worst **train accident** in the country's history.

Weather conditions were bad on Saturday, June 6, 1981, as a monsoon raged over the village of Mansi in the northeastern state of Bihar, India. The train was loaded with hundreds of riders, including some riding on the roofs of the packed wooden and metal cars. Some officials estimated that thousands of people were crammed onto the train—a common occurrence in India.

As the train traveled onto a bridge, the engineer reportedly saw a cow standing on the tracks. The engineer slammed on the brakes to avoid hitting the animal, but the tracks were wet and the roadbed soft and muddy from the storm's heavy rain. Instead of stopping, seven of the nine cars on the train slammed into each other and derailed. The cars fell off the bridge and plunged

into the raging waters of the Bagmati River below. The cars quickly sank, along with hundreds of passengers. There was no sign of survivors.

The locomotive and one car remained on the track, and eighty-three passengers were able to escape and run for help. Within hours, divers, soldiers, and villagers were on the scene, searching for survivors. But none were found. Over the next few days, divers pulled 268 bodies from the rain-swollen river. Hundreds more were missing, but their bodies were never recovered. The chief minister of Bihar called the accident the "biggest and worst in living memory."

The bodies of the victims were cremated in a large service on the banks of the river. Meanwhile, thousands of relatives camped out in tents while they tried to find out if their loved ones had survived.

The minister of railways and other government officials insisted that the accident had happened due to a gust of wind. However, there was no evidence of wind damage to any of the surrounding buildings or structures, and local weather stations did not record any strong winds at the time of the crash. Survivors told a different story, describing how the engineer had seen a cow on the tracks and braked to avoid hitting it. Bihar's rural development minister agreed, saying the accident had been caused by a "sudden application of the brakes." The cow may have been saved, but its life came at a cost of hundreds of innocent victims.

◆ Bridges and walkways can look sturdy and safe even if they are not structurally sound. If a walkway is poorly designed, it can collapse no matter how strong it seems or how much it cost to build.

The **Hyatt Regency Hotel** in **Kansas City**, Missouri, opened on July 1, 1980, and cost $50 million to build. One of its most impressive features was a five-story lobby connected by two **sky bridges** on the second and fourth floors.

On the evening of July 17, 1981, about fifteen hundred people were dancing or having dinner in a ballroom underneath the walkways. Above the dance floor, people walked across the skyways or stood on the bridges overlooking the dancers. Suddenly, as one witness reported, "there was a rumbling sound, exactly like a rolling clap of thunder outside." The fourth-floor walkway suddenly gave way and fell onto the second-floor walkway. Then, both bridges

crashed down into the lobby in a tangle of twisted steel and broken glass.

The hotel was evacuated as rescue workers rushed to the scene. One police officer reported seeing "arms and legs sticking out all over" from under the debris. Others compared the scene to a war zone.

The collapse caused several natural gas leaks, and rescuers feared the entire forty-story building might explode. The fear of leaks also prevented crews from using electric saws and burning torches to cut through debris. However, utility workers managed to stop the leaks, allowing rescuers to use their equipment to save people trapped in the debris. Part of the rescue effort included ripping out the metal frames of the lobby's plate-glass windows to allow cranes to enter and remove large steel girders and heavy chunks of concrete.

An exhibition hall in another part of the hotel was turned into a temporary morgue as workers pulled out body after body. Hundreds more victims were rushed to area hospitals. Although the original death toll was 43, many more died in hospitals over the next few days. The final death toll was 114. Approximately two hundred more were injured.

Teams of experts arrived at the hotel to determine what had caused the fourth-floor bridge to collapse. Seven months later, a federal investigation announced that a design change before construction had caused the disaster. Although the materials and workmanship of the hotel were not at fault, the steel poles and beams that connected the 75-foot-long bridge to the ceiling simply were not strong enough to hold the weight of the bridge and the people on it. This miscalculation caused one of the worst engineering disasters in U.S. history.

◆ Combine a heavy snow-storm, a traffic jam on a bridge, an icy river, and pilot error, and you have everything in place for a tragic disaster.

On January 13, 1982, it was a snowy day in Washington, DC. Schools, offices, and government buildings had closed early because of the storm, and the roads were packed with people trying to get home. The snow had also closed the Ronald Reagan Washington National Airport that morning. Although it reopened at noon, there were many delays as snowplows tried to keep the runway clear.

Air Florida Flight 90 was scheduled to leave the airport at 2:15 p.m. for a nonstop flight to Fort Lauderdale, Florida. Because of weather conditions, the flight didn't leave the gate until 3:30 p.m. While it waited, the plane was **deiced** to clean off its wings.

By the time Flight 90 was cleared for takeoff, shortly before four o'clock, it had been almost an hour since the last deicing. Despite this, the captain did not turn on the plane's deicing system. Instead, he pulled the plane up close behind another flight awaiting takeoff, allowing the first plane's exhaust to melt the snow and ice on Flight 90's wings. However, this procedure only blew melted snow farther back on the plane, where it quickly refroze.

As soon as Flight 90 took off, the pilot and crew realized that something was wrong. The plane's nose pulled up, but the craft did not gain altitude. Instead, the plane stalled, then crashed into the northbound side of the **Fourteenth Street Bridge**, also called the Rochambeau Bridge, crushing several cars that were stuck in a huge traffic jam caused by the storm. Then, the plane fell into the icy **Potomac River** and sank in about thirty feet of water.

Many passengers were killed instantly by the crash or drowned when they became trapped inside the plane underwater. Only half a dozen people made it to the surface, where they struggled to stay alive in the frigid water. Although police helicopters rushed to the scene, only five people were pulled from the water. Seventy-four passengers and four motorists on the bridge were killed.

One of the dead passengers was Arland Williams. He became a hero when news reports described how he passed life vests and flotation devices from rescue helicopters to victims struggling in the water. On two occasions, Williams passed a lifeline from the helicopter to other passengers, allowing them to be pulled to safety. When a helicopter returned for Williams, he had disappeared beneath the icy waters. To honor him, the Rochambeau Bridge was renamed the Arland D. Williams Jr. Memorial Bridge.

It did not take crash investigators long to figure out what had happened to Flight 90. They found that the crew's failure to deice the plane caused large amounts of ice and snow to accumulate in the engines. This made the plane too heavy to fly and cost the lives of seventy-eight innocent victims.

An innocent misunder-standing or a deliberate act of aggression? That was the question on everyone's mind after the former **Soviet Union** shot down a commercial airliner in 1983.

Korean Air Lines Flight 007 (KAL007) left New York City at 12:24 a.m. on the morning of August 31. It was headed for **Seoul, South Korea**, with 246 passengers and twenty-three crew members. The plane stopped in Anchorage,

Alaska, to refuel and take on a new crew. Its new captain, **Chun Byung-in**, was one of the airline's best pilots, and he had flown the route between Alaska and South Korea many times.

For some reason, however, Byung-in did not keep Flight 007 on its assigned course. Instead, the plane mistakenly headed a few miles north of the normal route, traveling over several military bases in the Soviet Union in restricted airspace.

Soviet air traffic controllers quickly spotted the jet and began tracking it. For two and a half hours, the Soviets watched the plane. As Flight 007 flew over **Sakhalin Island**, six Soviet planes intercepted it. One of the Soviet pilots fired 120 warning shells at the plane. Then, under orders from the Soviet air defense commander, the plane launched two missiles. One hit the Korean plane's engines and the plane exploded. All 269 people on board were killed.

The American and South Korean governments reacted angrily. **U.S. Secretary of State George Shultz** said there was "no excuse whatsoever for this appalling act." He also said there was no evidence that the Soviets had either warned the plane that it was in Soviet airspace or that they gave the Korean plane a chance to land safely. Korean Air Lines officials insisted the plane had not gone off course. More than ten thousand angry South Koreans marched in protest, while governments around the world condemned the action.

The Soviets responded by saying the jet was on a spy mission. The fact that it was clearly a commercial plane did not seem to matter because they said it was "easy to turn a civilian type of plane into one for military use."

As the governments traded accusations, wreckage and body parts began washing up on the coast of northern Japan. Both Soviet and U.S. warships were sent to the area to retrieve pieces of the plane from the water.

The Soviets found the airplane's flight data recorder and cockpit voice recorder but refused to release them to authorities. Finally, ten years later, the recorders were given to the **International Civil Aviation Organization**, but the tapes were so garbled that no one could understand what had been said.

After a lengthy investigation, the International Civil Aviation Organization determined that Flight 007 was accidentally shot down by the Soviets. The American government accepted this official explanation. However, many people still believe that the Korean plane was on a spy mission, and that the pilot deliberately sent the plane off course to observe Soviet air and military bases. The true story of the destruction of Flight 007 probably will never be revealed.

Famines are nothing new in **sub-Saharan Africa**, the area below the Sahara Desert. In 1983, a famine began in **Ethiopia** and the **Sudan**. Before it was over, more than a million people had died, despite efforts from some unlikely places.

The famine in the 1980s had a number of causes. This area grows almost all of its own food, so a lack of rainfall can cause catastrophic crop failures. Because the land is farmed and grazed so heavily, trees and grass are lost, and the land is unable to hold what little moisture there is. Slowly, over time, the Sahara Desert advanced, turning the once-fertile countryside into a huge bowl of sand.

Constant civil and tribal warfare and corrupt governments also lead to famine. People are displaced from their land as a result of the fighting, and food supplies do not reach refugee camps in time. Governments hoard food instead of distributing it to the poor or use aid money for purposes other than relief efforts.

By 1984, the **United Nations** reported that up to seven million Ethiopians were in danger of starvation. Many who did not starve to death were so weak that they had become sick and died of disease. In 1988, an outbreak of measles killed almost all children under two years old in the Sudan.

The United States and other governments sent millions of dollars in aid and food to Ethiopia and the Sudan. However, it often took several weeks for the food to be distributed. Meanwhile, eight to ten people died every day.

One night in 1984, a British rock star named Bob Geldof saw a television documentary about the famine. Geldof was shocked by the images and flew to Ethiopia to see the situation firsthand. When he came back to London, he wrote a song about the famine called "Do They Know It's Christmas?" Then, he persuaded dozens of other British rock stars to donate their time to record the song, which became a chart-topping hit in Europe and the United States, raising more than $5 million in famine relief.

Next Geldof organized **Live Aid**. On July 13, 1985, two benefit concerts were held simultaneously in London and Philadelphia. More than fifty of the biggest music stars of the '80s performed for free. The broadcast was televised to 1.4 billion people around the world and raised almost $50 million. Geldof, who previously had a reputation for being self-centered, said: "Maybe I was given my arrogance and ego to do this."

With help from Live Aid, other charities, and governments from around the world, the famine in Ethiopia and the Sudan eased by 1988. But their efforts were not enough to save at least 1.2 million people, including thousands of children, who died during the famine. Corrupt governments, constant fighting, and poor farming conditions continue to plague sub-Saharan Africa today, meaning that the days of starvation and disease are not over.

For thousands of people in **Bhopal, India**, the **Union Carbide Pesticide Plant** provided needed jobs and economic stimulus. But early in the morning of December 3, 1984, the chemical plant brought death.

Union Carbide was one of the world's leading producers of chemicals. Like many industries, it moved some of its plants to developing countries like India because it was cheaper to operate there. Sadly, some of these chemical plants were outdated and lacked safety features.

The Union Carbide plant in Bhopal opened in 1969. In 1979, it began producing methyl isocyanate (MIC), a deadly gas used to make pesticides. The gas was stored in three huge tanks.

Conditions at the Bhopal plant were not good. The equipment was old and not properly maintained. One of the tanks had a faulty valve and was overfilled. On the day of the disaster, many of the workers and their supervisors were new and unfamiliar with proper safety procedures.

At 9:30 p.m. on the evening of December 2, a worker turned on the water to clean out a section of pipe that filtered MIC before it went into the tank. Water reacts violently with MIC, and the flow caused the pressure inside the tank to rise. However, no one paid much attention to the pressure readings because the "instruments often didn't work," according to one supervisor.

By 12:40 a.m. on December 3, a deadly white cloud of MIC burst out of the plant, and wind carried it into the crowded slums surrounding the plant. Although some emergency sirens sounded, others had not worked for several years. Many residents who heard the sirens assumed that it was a false alarm. Others were asleep and had no chance to escape the deadly gas.

Victims who did wake up found themselves choking and blinded. Many dropped dead as they tried to run away. Thousands rushed toward a hill, thinking that they could climb above the gas. "There were cars, bicycles, auto rickshaws—anything that could move on the road trying to get up the hill," said one survivor. "I saw people just collapsing by the side of the road."

Hospitals were soon overwhelmed with victims and reported as many as one death per minute. Emergency clinics were set up in fields and along the roads. Thousands of bodies lay in Bhopal's streets. Birds and other animals had also died, and there was no sound except for trucks driving through the city to pick up corpses.

More than two thousand people died in Bhopal, making it the deadliest chemical disaster in history. At least two hundred thousand more were injured. Many were permanently blinded or disabled by the gas.

Although Union Carbide claimed that the plant had been sabotaged, an investigation concluded that the cause was human error and out-of-date equipment. India's government sued Union Carbide, and the company eventually paid $470 million in damages. The accident left people around the world wondering about the safety of chemical plants in their own backyards.

On August 12, 1985, it was a busy travel day in Japan. Thousands of people were heading home to celebrate a traditional midsummer holiday. For 520 people on a Japan Airlines (JAL) **Boeing 747SR**, the journey would end in death.

Japan Airlines Flight 123 left Tokyo at 6:15 p.m., heading for **Osaka, Japan**, about 250 miles away. Although passengers did not know it, the plane had made a rough landing at Osaka's airport seven years earlier, which damaged the lower rear portion of the plane. The plane had supposedly been fixed, though, and was put back into service.

Thirteen minutes into the flight, passengers and crew heard a loud noise in the back of the plane. Cabin pressure dropped, and the nose of the plane was forced up. Even worse, the craft's control system had stopped responding. The pilot told air traffic controllers that he was in trouble and was losing control of the plane. "We may be finished," he said. Meanwhile, the crew told the passengers to prepare for an emergency landing.

At 6:57 p.m., half an hour after the pilot reported problems, the craft crashed into the side of Mount Ogura, a 6,929-foot-tall mountain about seventy miles northwest of Tokyo. The impact caused a tremendous explosion and set fire to acres of forest. An eyewitness described seeing "a big flame... followed by a white smoke which turned into a black mushroom-like cloud."

The crash site was so remote that it took fourteen hours for rescue teams to arrive on the scene. They were confronted with a grim sight as only four people had survived the crash. The crash killed five hundred twenty people, making it the worst single-plane accident in history.

Investigators studied the wreckage, much of which was burned or buried in the mountain. Then, the Japanese Navy found part of the plane's tail in Sagami Bay, eighty miles away from the crash site. The tail had apparently fallen off the plane shortly after takeoff.

Investigators soon figured out what happened. When the plane had been repaired seven years earlier, a double line of rivets should have been used to attach the back of the passenger compartment to the tail. Instead, only a single line was used. Seven years of metal fatigue and stress finally took a toll on August 12, when that section of the plane gave way.

Although Boeing had repaired the plane and took full responsibility for the accident, Japan Airlines officials also felt the blame. Shortly after the investigation was complete, the airline's president and two other executives resigned. On September 21, the crash took another victim, when a Japan Airlines maintenance official died by suicide. He left a note reading simply: "I atone with my death."

Earthquakes are nothing new in Mexico. During the twentieth century alone, the country experienced more than forty major earthquakes, with the most powerful one striking early on September 19.

The quake actually occurred off the Pacific coast of Mexico, sending shock waves across the country. **Mexico City** was two hundred fifty miles away from the epicenter of the earthquake,

which measured 8.0 on the Richter scale. The city shook violently for three minutes. Hundreds of buildings collapsed immediately. Residents in buildings that had not collapsed described the buildings as swinging back and forth, while furniture flew across the rooms and windows shattered. Walls cracked, streets split open, and smoke and dust filled the air. The twelve-story Hotel Principiado collapsed, killing more than one hundred people. At least eight hundred people were killed when an apartment building crumbled into a pile of concrete.

The suburbs outside the city also suffered devastation. Twenty-five people were killed in Ciudad Guzmán when a cathedral collapsed during Mass. Survivors described how "the streets split open as people ran in panic."

Mexico's army and police force rushed to the disaster to control the damage, rescue the trapped and injured, and collect the dead. Specially trained workers and search dogs arrived from the United States and Europe to locate bodies in the debris. Workers and residents walked through the streets wearing surgical masks or handkerchiefs over their mouths and noses to keep out the dust and the smell of decaying bodies. Officials struggled to restore water, electricity, and telephone lines as more than ten aftershocks hit the city.

There were some amazing stories of survival. A newborn baby was placed in an incubator seconds before the hospital collapsed in the quake. More than fifty-five hours later, rescuers discovered the incubator wedged under a steel beam. The incubator was dented, but the baby was alive and unharmed inside.

Thirty-six hours after the first quake, another earthquake struck the city. This quake measured 7.6 on the Richter scale. Dozens of rescue workers were injured, and many buildings that had been damaged in the first earthquake collapsed.

The Mexico City earthquake killed ninety-five hundred people, injured thirty thousand, and left fifty thousand homeless. Four hundred buildings were destroyed and seven hundred more were seriously damaged.

Mexico learned from this disaster. An earthquake **alarm system** was installed along the **fault line** where the 1985 earthquake took place. This system now sends a message to schools, government offices, apartment buildings, and radio and television stations anytime an earthquake measuring 6.0 or greater is felt. In 1995, the system faced its most serious test when a 7.2 quake occurred on the fault line. Residents of Mexico City were alerted and evacuated their homes 72 seconds before the earthquake hit the city.

As the **space shuttle** *Challenger* prepared to blast off from Cape Canaveral, Florida, on January 28, 1986, everyone knew that it was no ordinary flight. For the first time in the history of space travel, an ordinary civilian—**Christa McAuliffe**, a high school social studies teacher from New Hampshire—would be a crew member. Originally, the *Challenger* was supposed to blast into space on Saturday, January 25, 1986. But bad weather forced the **National Aeronautics and Space Administration (NASA)** to postpone the flight. The same thing happened on Sunday and Monday.

By Tuesday, January 28, both NASA and the American people were very anxious to get the *Challenger* into space. The weather that day was clear but very cold. NASA decided to go ahead with the liftoff.

Millions watched on TV as the *Challenger* rose from the launchpad into the sky. Then, just 74 seconds after liftoff, flames emerged from the solid rocket booster on the bottom right portion of the shuttle. In the blink of an eye, the *Challenger* exploded.

"Obviously a major malfunction," said the voice of mission control. In fact, the explosion was the worst disaster in the history of American space exploration, and the first time American astronauts had been killed during a spaceflight.

Search crews rushed to the Atlantic Ocean. Although pieces of the shuttle and its rockets continued to fall into the ocean for an hour, the bodies of the seven crew members were never recovered.

A few days after the accident, an investigative committee began looking into what had happened. Meanwhile, scientists gathered the wreckage of the shuttle and put the spacecraft back together inside a hangar at the space center.

The investigative committee published a 256-page report that blamed the explosion on **cracked O-rings** on the right solid rocket booster. An O-ring is a piece of rubber that holds two parts of the booster rocket together. When the O-rings cracked, fire escaped from the rocket and burned through the support that held the rocket to the fuel tank. This caused the rocket to hit the fuel tank, creating the tremendous explosion.

The O-rings failed because of the cold weather at the time of the launch. NASA had been warned of this possibility, but they were so eager to get the *Challenger* into space that they decided to take a chance and go ahead with the launch.

The *Challenger* disaster led to many changes in shuttle design and astronaut training. Because many people believed that the astronauts had survived the initial explosion and died due to secondary issues caused by the disaster, evacuation procedures were improved to give future astronauts a better chance at escaping.

Finally, on September 29, 1988—thirty-two months after the *Challenger* disaster—**space shuttle *Discovery*** lifted off from Cape Canaveral. This time, the shuttle launch went perfectly, but the American people would never forget the terrible sight of the *Challenger* explosion on that cold January morning.

The Soviet government called the **Chernobyl nuclear power station** a model of nuclear safety. However, many scientists thought that the plant had been built too fast and that the reactor's poor design could lead to widespread disaster. They were right.

On April 25, 1986, Chernobyl's engineers turned off a generator in reactor Unit 4 to test how much energy it produced as it was shutting down. As part of the test, the reactor's automatic shutdown systems and the emergency core cooling system were also shut down.

As the power fell to very low levels, reactions in the **core** became hard to control. Workers tried to increase the power by removing some of the safety rods from the core. This caused steam to accumulate and become unsafe.

Shortly after one o'clock in the morning on April 26, two huge steam explosions destroyed the nuclear core. The one-thousand-ton-concrete and steel roof of the reactor blew off, and flames shot fifteen hundred feet into the air. The explosion released about seven tons of radioactive material.

A radioactive cloud spread over the nearby town of Pripyat. Residents were ordered to stay inside their homes and keep all the doors and windows closed, but the forty-nine thousand people were not evacuated for thirty-six hours after the accident. By May 2, though, 179 other towns and approximately one hundred thirty-five thousand people were also evacuated.

About thirty people were killed at Chernobyl, including firefighters exposed to huge doses of radiation as they battled the flames. About five hundred more people were hospitalized for severe radiation exposure.

To stop radiation leaks, the damaged reactor was entombed in three hundred thousand tons of concrete. Workers also removed contaminated soil and cleaned radiation from thousands of buildings. Still, most areas around the plant were too unsafe for people to ever return.

Over the next few weeks, radiation spread all over the world. Europe was affected within days. Within a week, the radiation reached Japan, and two weeks later, North America recorded high levels of radiation. Since the radiation weakened the farther it spread, Asia and the Americas were not seriously affected.

Things were quite different, however, in the Ukraine, Finland, Sweden, Denmark, and Norway. Some farmers were burned or suffered radiation sickness when heavy rains washed radiation onto their fields. Crops were inedible as well as milk and meat from animals that had grazed on radioactive grass.

The concrete coffin around the reactor eventually began deteriorating, and in 2016, a new structure built to contain the remains, called the New Safe Confinement, was put into place. Even today, the dangers of Chernobyl's **meltdown** remain. The ground, air, and water are still radioactive and potentially deadly. Doctors recorded a large increase in thyroid cancer among Soviet children in 1986, and since then between twenty thousand and two hundred thousand people have died from cancers caused by Chernobyl's radiation exposure. The effects of the explosion may never completely end.

Can lakes erupt? They can if they are filled with volcanic gases, causing disasters that are both unusual and deadly.

Lake Nyos is located about 375 miles northwest of Cameroon's capital city of Yaounde. The lake rests on a crater of a dormant volcano. **Geothermal springs** from the volcano feed the lake and make the water warm. They also fill the lake with **carbon dioxide**.

On August 21, something unusual happened near Lake Nyos. Up to seventeen hundred people simply and mysteriously died. Whole villages were wiped out, and thousands of cattle and other animals collapsed in fields. None of the bodies had any sign of injury. It was clear that death had come quickly and suddenly.

Scientists rushed to the area. They discovered that all the victims had suffocated in a deadly cloud of carbon dioxide. The carbon dioxide came from the lake in what

is known as a **limnic eruption**, covering the area with a poisonous fog. This was not the first time such a thing had happened in Cameroon. Two years earlier, thirty-six people had died in a similar incident at another lake.

Researchers discovered that recent heavy rains had cooled the surface water, causing it to sink beneath the warm, gas-laden water at the bottom of the lake. As the warm water rose, it released carbon dioxide bubbles, which created a fizzy gas explosion like from a can of soda being opened. Finally, two hundred sixty-four thousand tons of carbon dioxide erupted from the lake and floated down onto the houses and pastures of the village below.

Survivors around Lake Nyos were quickly evacuated from the area and resettled in government camps. However, most were unhappy with their lives there. In time, they returned to the fertile land around the lake, despite the danger.

The 1986 incident was terrifying because it was so unexpected and sudden. But scientists had even more frightening news: another deadly incident could happen again, as gas pressure continued to build up in Lake Nyos.

Scientists recommended several procedures to remove gas from the lake and prevent another eruption and terrible loss of life. Some suggested draining the lake but that would not have been practical. The best option was to lower a pipe to the bottom of the lake and pump out the gas. The pipe would work like a straw, sucking up small amounts of water and gas into the air where the gas could evaporate harmlessly. One such pipe was installed in Lake Nyos in 2001, and two more were added in 2011, thanks to funding from the **United Nations Development Programme**.

Sometimes, labor disputes can spark tragedies. On New Year's Eve in 1986, guests at a luxe hotel discovered just how deadly one employee's anger could be.

The management of the **Dupont Plaza Hotel** (now San Juan Marriott Resort & Stellaris Casino) in **San Juan, Puerto Rico**, had been trying to negotiate a new contract with employees, who were members of the **International Brotherhood of Teamsters**. On December 31, the teamsters decided to go on strike. Three of the employees—**Héctor Escudero Aponte**, **Armando Jiménez Rivera**, and **José Francisco Rivera López**—did not think that management would take the union's demands seriously even if they went on strike, so they decided to take matters into their own hands.

Around 3:00 p.m., the three picked up cans of Sterno, a fuel used for cooking, from the kitchen. They made their way to a storage room just beside the ballroom, where some new furniture was stacked in piles and wrapped in plastic. They lit the Sterno and placed it next to one of the piles. Escudero Aponte later said that he only meant to start "a small fire that would damage the personal property of the hotel."

The "small fire" quickly got out of control. Fed by the plastic wrap, the blaze roared up the walls and into the nearby casino. Patrons smelled smoke, but by the time they realized the danger, it was too late to escape.

Unable to flee through the smoke-filled halls, many people in the casino smashed the floor-to-ceiling windows that overlooked the pool and jumped out. Several patrons leaped into the pool to extinguish their burning clothing, while others lay bleeding from flying glass.

The building had no sprinkler system, so the fire spread quickly. Burning plastic made the smoke especially toxic. Some people died while still sitting in chairs in the lobby as they were so quickly overcome by the poisonous smoke.

Guests in the rooms above the casino were trapped in by the thick smoke and flames, which spread through the air conditioning vents. Many died in stairwells when the doors locked behind them. Others were lucky enough to find rooms with balconies. They wrapped wet towels over their faces and hung out the windows until firefighters rescued them several hours later.

Many guests fled to the roof, hoping to be rescued by helicopters. At first, only one helicopter was on the scene, but it could not land because the roof was not flat. Instead, the pilot, Pat Walker, placed one landing skid on the roof while a police officer pulled people into the helicopter. Walker rescued twenty-one people before larger military helicopters arrived to help.

The fire was brought under control by 7:00 p.m. that night, but it was days before all the victims could be identified. Ninety-six people had died, and hundreds more were injured. The three men were convicted of murder. Jiménez Rivera was sentenced to seventy-five years in prison, and both Escudero Aponte and Rivera López were sentenced to ninety-nine years each.

For people who live on islands, ships are the easiest and cheapest way to travel. Unfortunately, many of these ships are overcrowded and unsafe. In 1987, these conditions are what led to a tremendous loss of life in the Philippines.

The ferry **motor vessel (MV)** *Doña Paz* left Leyte Island in the Philippines on Sunday, December 20, 1987. The ship was designed to carry about fifteen hundred passengers, but it was jammed packed with about three thousand people on their way to spend Christmas with family and friends in the Philippine capital city of Manila. Conditions were so uncomfortable that hundreds of passengers lay on mats in hallways or sat shoulder to shoulder on the ship's three decks.

The *Doña Paz* sailed into the **Tablas Strait**, a busy shipping passage. At 10:00 p.m. that night, only one apprentice officer was piloting the ship while other officers watched television inside the ship. Suddenly, the ferry collided head-on with an oil tanker, **motor tanker (MT)** *Vector.* The impact ripped open the *Vector* and ignited the eighty-three hundred barrels of oil on board. Flaming oil

poured down on the *Doña Paz* and set the water around the ships on fire. Both ships sank quickly.

The fire and smoke spread so quickly that most people on board the *Doña Paz* had no chance to escape. Others drowned or were burned to death by flaming oil as they fell or jumped into the ocean. "I went to a window to see what had happened, and I saw the sea in flames," said Paquito Osabel, one of the few survivors. "And I shouted to my companions to get ready, that there is fire. The fire spread rapidly, and there were flames everywhere. People were screaming and jumping. The smoke was terrible."

Another passenger ship, the **MS Don Claudio**, was also in the Tablas Strait. Crew members searched the water for survivors, but only about twenty-five people were rescued.

The next day, hundreds of bodies began washing ashore on nearby beaches. Thousands more were lost forever in the sea. At least three thousand people died in the collision. It was the deadliest peacetime maritime disaster in history.

Ferries in the Philippines have long had a reputation for being unsafe. In just fifteen years between 1972 and 1987, 117 ships sank, fifty-three had fires, and eighty were involved in collisions. Unfortunately, many ships remain largely unregulated and overcrowded, regularly endangering many innocent lives.

When disaster strikes, entire towns and communities can disappear. That was the case when an earthquake struck **Armenia**, then a part of the Soviet Union, one cold December day.

The earthquake struck at 11:41 a.m. on Wednesday morning, December 7, 1988, and measured 6.9 on the Richter scale. "It was like a slow-motion movie," recalled one survivor who was working in a factory when the earthquake hit. "There was a concrete panel slowly falling down." Another survivor said, "There was a loud humming noise, then steam burst out of the ground, buildings began to rock like boats, and it was as though the earth was boiling."

The quake destroyed two-thirds of Leninakan, Armenia's second largest city. The town of Spitak, which had sixteen thousand residents, was leveled, and neighboring villages were also wiped out. "I have never seen anything like this," said **Yevgen Chazov**, the Soviet health minister, after he toured the area by airplane. "The scope is just catastrophic."

Soviet **President Mikhail Gorbachev** was in the United States when the quake hit, and he quickly rushed home when he heard about the disaster. Gorbachev was introducing more freedoms and a new openness to Soviet society at that time. Unlike government policy in previous disasters, the Soviets admitted how bad things were and welcomed foreign aid. Within days, firefighters, doctors, and specially trained search-and-rescue dogs had arrived in Armenia. They came from forty-six countries around the world, in the greatest outpouring of foreign aid since the end of World War II.

Tents, blankets, medical supplies, and excavation equipment also came from countries around the world. A "helicopter bridge" was set up to take the injured to hospitals in other parts of the Soviet Union. Survivors huddled in the bitter cold, seeking shelter in tents or in the remains of damaged buildings.

The earthquake killed at least twenty-five thousand people, although some estimates stated more than fifty-five thousand had died. At least twelve thousand were injured, four hundred thousand were left homeless, and fifty-eight towns and villages were destroyed. The area is still recovering from the disaster today.

Many of the houses and office buildings in the area were poorly constructed and were no match for the violently shaking earth, which led to the high death toll. Thousands of buildings collapsed, including tall apartment buildings. "Practically all apartment buildings with nine floors or more were destroyed," reported one survivor in Spitak. Soviet officials blamed the poor construction on previous government policies.

The openness to help from other countries was new for the Soviet Union, which undoubtedly saved many lives. In addition, scientists used information gathered in Armenia to design new monitoring stations. As one scientist put it, "A safer world awaits our resolve to act together."

A few days before Christmas, a **terrorist bomb** devastated the small farming village of Lockerbie, Scotland, United Kingdom. But the bomb was not planted on the ground. Instead, the blast ripped apart a plane high above in the sky.

Pan Am Flight 103 took off from Heathrow Airport in London at 6:25 p.m. on December 21, 1988, bound for New York City. The flight carried 258 passengers and crew. Many were traveling to visit family and friends for the holidays. Among the passengers were more than thirty students from Syracuse University in Upstate New York, returning home to the United States after a semester in London.

Fifty-two minutes after takeoff, the Boeing 747 was flying at thirty-one thousand feet over Scotland. Without warning, a bomb in the plane's baggage compartment exploded. The plane blew apart and fell to the ground. The crash was so powerful that seismographs fourteen miles away recorded a tremor.

Flaming wreckage crashed down on Lockerbie, killing twelve residents and destroying several houses and a service station. The impact of the huge engines, fuel tanks, and wings of the plane created a huge crater in the earth. Bodies from the plane were strewn along the ground and on the rooftops.

"The plane came down four hundred yards from my house," reported Bob Glaster, a retired police officer. "There was a ball of fire three hundred feet into the air, and debris was falling from the sky. When the smoke cleared a little, I could see bodies in the road. At least one dozen houses were destroyed." Another resident eyewitness reported, "The whole road was ablaze."

Along with the twelve victims in Lockerbie, all 258 passengers on board the plane were killed. Wreckage and bodies were found miles from the crash site. Smaller items, such as mail, papers, clothing, jewelry, and personal belongings of the passengers, turned up seventy miles away.

Investigators quickly placed the blame on a bomb. The plane had taken off from Frankfurt, Germany, earlier on December 21. Frankfurt's airport was notorious for its poor security, and many smugglers were able to ship illegal drugs out of that airport. Now, it seemed that terrorists had taken advantage of the poor security to place a bomb on Flight 103. The bomb had been made of a soft plastic explosive called **Semtex** and placed inside a tape recorder that was packed in a suitcase. The suitcase was not matched with a passenger on board the plane when it left Frankfurt, one of the notorious security lapses there at the time. Investigators believed that Flight 103 was bombed in retaliation for an incident on July 3, 1988, when an American warship in the **Persian Gulf** shot down an Iranian jetliner, killing 340 people.

After years of international investigations, two terrorists from **Libya** were charged with bombing Flight 103. In April 1999, these men were finally put on trial at the **International Court of Justice** in The Hague. One man was acquitted, but the other was convicted and sentenced to life in a Scottish prison in 2001.

◆ Not all disasters kill people. Environmental disasters, such as the crash of the **Exxon *Valdez***, harm the natural world and claim thousands of animal lives.

The Exxon *Valdez* carried oil from the **Trans-Alaska Pipeline** in Valdez, Alaska, to Long Beach, California. At 9:26 p.m. on March 23, 1989, the tanker left Valdez filled with fifty-three million gallons of oil.

After the ship entered **Prince William Sound**, Captain **Joseph Hazelwood** saw **icebergs** in the water and turned left to avoid them. Before he went to his cabin for the night, Hazelwood told third mate Gregory Cousins to place the *Exxon Valdez* back on its correct course. But when Cousins tried to do so, the tanker did not respond. Instead, it headed straight toward **Bligh Reef** and crashed into the rocks at 12:04 a.m. on March 24.

The crash ripped open about six hundred feet of the ship's hull and damaged eight of its thirteen cargo tanks. Oil gushed into the sound, spilling about two hundred thousand gallons of oil per minute.

The **Exxon Corporation**, the **Alyeska Pipeline Service Company**, and the **U.S. Coast Guard** sent workers and equipment to clean up the oil. More than ten thousand volunteers also arrived from all over the world. Crews used skimmers to pick up oil from the water and pump it away, and then they placed plastic booms in the water to keep the oil from spreading. But their efforts were no match for the eleven million gallons of oil in the water.

The oil spill was especially toxic to animals. Workers quickly put up booms around fisheries in the sound to protect fifteen million salmon, while state officials closed fishing areas to prevent people from eating contaminated fish.

Scientists estimated that as many as two hundred seventy thousand birds were killed when oil made their bodies too heavy to float and ruined their waterproof feathers. Workers also found more than twenty-eight hundred dead otters.

The **National Transportation Safety Board (NTSB)** blamed human error for the crash. The NTSB said Captain Hazelwood failed to provide proper supervision and that Cousins was too tired and overworked to guide the tanker properly. The NTSB also blamed Exxon for not training the crew properly and making them work too many hours.

In 1990, Hazelwood was sentenced to one thousand hours of community service cleaning beaches in the Prince William Sound. Hazelwood also paid $50,000 toward the cost of cleaning up the oil.

Exxon paid more than $2 billion to clean up the oil spill. The company was also fined $150 million, virtually the most ever paid for environmental damage.

Today, oil companies have better plans to deal with oil spills. Oil tankers also must be built better to withstand damage in a crash, and crew members must have more training.

Parts of Prince William Sound's shoreline remained saturated with oil for decades. Scientists also discovered genetic damage to salmon, herring, and other fish in the waters. Prince William Sound, its fishing industry, and its residents would never be the same.

Some disasters strike quickly and suddenly. Others take their time, spreading death and destruction even though everyone knows they are coming. Hurricanes are a prime example of a disaster that should not take anyone by surprise.

Like many hurricanes, **Hurricane Hugo** formed in the warm waters off the western coast of Africa. It crossed the Atlantic Ocean and made landfall on the **U.S. Virgin Islands**. The islands of St. Thomas and St. Croix were pounded by 100-mile-per-hour winds. Roofs were torn off and power was knocked out. The **U.S. National Guard** was called in to stop looting in St. Croix, where most of the residents had been evacuated to emergency shelters.

Other islands were also severely affected. Eighty people were injured in Guadeloupe, and four thousand more were left homeless by the storm. Power, telephone service, and radio and television broadcasts were also cut off.

After it finished with Guadeloupe, Hugo turned its fury on **Puerto Rico**. People who lived in low-lying areas were evacuated to a stadium in the city of Mayaguez. Others sought shelter in churches, schools, and other public buildings as high winds and heavy rains overturned cars, ripped roofs off houses, and cut off power and water supplies. A total of twenty-six people were killed in Puerto Rico and on other Caribbean islands.

Then it was the United States' turn. Just after midnight on September 22, Hugo slammed into **Charleston, South Carolina**.

Winds up to 135 mph and a 17-foot-high tidal surge destroyed thirty buildings and flooded streets throughout the area. The **historic Fort Sumter** was heavily damaged when a 17-foot-high wave washed over it. "There's just destruction everywhere," said Charleston's mayor, who called the storm "a disaster of extraordinary dimensions."

Charleston was a historic city filled with beautiful mansions that were more than one hundred years old. The storm damaged many of these houses as well as expensive, new homes built along the water. Harder hit, though, were Charleston's old trees. Hundreds of huge oaks and other trees were uprooted and smashed throughout the city.

Hugo's devastation also struck islands off the coast of South Carolina. Houses were blown off their foundations and boats were pushed out of the water to lie two and three feet deep on the beach. Pawleys Island was literally cut in two by a 100-foot-wide stretch of water, and two beachfront houses were washed into a marsh four hundred feet away.

Despite its destruction, Hugo quickly lost power once it was over land and away from the warm waters of the ocean. The storm drifted over Pennsylvania, Western New York, and Ohio, before finally dying out in Canada. In its wake, Hugo left fifty-four people dead (including twenty-eight in the United States) and more than $7 billion worth of damage in America, making it one of the most expensive storms to ever hit the country.

It was around 5:00 p.m. on Tuesday evening, October 17, 1989. The third game of the World Series was about to start in Candlestick Park in **San Francisco**. As viewers all over the country tuned in to watch the game, television cameras suddenly shook violently. Announcer Al Michaels yelled, "We're having an earth—." Then the power went out. A 7.1 quake had just occurred along the **Loma Prieta** segment of the **San Andreas Fault**, just sixty miles away.

The baseball game was quickly postponed, and attention shifted to other parts of the city. It soon became clear that a disrupted sporting event was the least of San Francisco's worries. The **Marina district**, an area near San Francisco Bay, was heavily damaged. Apartment buildings collapsed, and witnesses saw several bodies in the ruins. Parts of the neighborhood had caught fire from ruptured gas lines, adding to the chaos and destruction. Combined with mud and sand, this area was built on top of rubble from the earthquake in 1906. During the earthquake in 1989, the movement of the earth caused the ground to liquefy underneath the buildings, which then collapsed.

The greatest damage, however, affected local highways. Fifty feet of the **San Francisco-Oakland Bay Bridge** collapsed, carrying several cars with it. Video cameras captured the eerie sight of one car driving right off the edge of the road. This footage was replayed over and over on television.

The scene was even worse on Interstate 880, or the **Nimitz Freeway**, which was an elevated highway in the nearby city of Oakland. A one-mile stretch of this road collapsed when its support columns fell, crushing cars and trapping hundreds of people in a pile of twisted metal and broken concrete. "It looked like a snake that had been hacked by an ax," said California Senator Alan Cranston when he saw the crushed roadway from a helicopter. "It was in bits and pieces." Rescue workers rushed to the scene and struggled to free seriously injured victims. The earthquake had struck at rush hour, when roads were very crowded, and several hundred cars were caught in the collapse.

Although original estimates of the death toll were as high as two hundred fifty, the final number was sixty-eight. Most of those had been on the Nimitz Freeway. About thirty-eight hundred people were injured, and eight thousand more were homeless. Seven counties were declared disaster areas, and more than one hundred thousand homes and businesses were damaged and destroyed.

Despite terrible hardships, life started returning to normal within weeks of the earthquake. However, it took years to rebuild all the housing units and damaged roadways. Engineers designed bridges that could better withstand earthquakes, hoping to avoid future disasters.

Even the World Series continued. When Game 3 was finally played at Oakland Coliseum, the American flag was flown at half-staff to honor the quake victims.

On March 25, 1990, it was the seventy-ninth anniversary of the **Triangle Shirtwaist Factory Fire** (see no. 18), the deadliest fire in New York City's history. That same night, another fire would put the city in mourning once more.

The **Happy Land social club** was located in a Honduran neighborhood in the **Bronx**. Hundreds of residents paid five dollars apiece and packed the club on weekends to dance, drink, and party. However, the club was illegal and did not follow safety guidelines. Patrons climbed a steep, narrow staircase to reach a windowless upstairs room that contained a dance floor and a bar. There were no fire alarms or sprinkler systems, and not enough exits.

During the early morning hours of Sunday, March 25, the club was packed with partygoers. Lydia Feliciano was working as a coat-check attendant when her ex-boyfriend, **Julio González**, showed up. The two got into an argument, and a security guard asked González to leave. Furious, González swore he would be back to shut down the club for good.

González found a plastic jug and walked to a nearby gas station. He filled the jug with gasoline and went back to the Happy Land around 3:30 a.m. González waited until no one was around, then poured a trail of gasoline from the door into the downstairs hallway, dropped a lighted match, and left.

The fire roared through the downstairs, and one of the security guards began yelling

"Fire!" At first, there was only a small amount of smoke upstairs, but the two DJs turned up the lights and told people to leave. However, the fire moved so quickly that the people upstairs had no chance to escape. Only three people, including the two DJs, would emerge from the second story.

By the time the fire department arrived on the scene at 3:44 a.m., it was too late. Nineteen people died of burns or smoke inhalation on the ground floor, while sixty-eight more were dead in the crowded, tiny room upstairs. They had died within seconds from suffocation and smoke inhalation. "It was shocking," said First Deputy Mayor Norman Steisel. "None of the bodies I saw showed signs of burns. They looked waxen." The disaster was the second-deadliest fire in New York City's history.

Eyewitnesses, including Lydia Feliciano and the club's security guard, told police about Julio González's behavior shortly before the fire. A few hours later, he was arrested and charged with eighty-seven counts of arson and eighty-seven counts of murder. In July 1991, González was found guilty on all charges and sentenced to twenty-five years to life in prison for each count.

The Happy Land social club fire focused attention on the city's illegal clubs. Although a police crackdown closed many of these locations, most soon reopened. Illegal social clubs still exist today, despite the dangers.

On Saturday, October 19, 1991, firefighters were called to the hills near **Oakland, California**, to put out a **brush fire**. Brush fires were common in the heavily wooded area during the dry fall season. Firefighters put out this blaze in about two hours. They did not realize that this ordinary fire would become one of the most devastating blazes in California history.

The next day, a fire crew returned to the scene to make sure there were no areas that were still smoldering. The crew found some embers and sprayed water on them.

Suddenly, the wind began to blow very hard. One ember jumped to a tree and started a new fire. The flames spread so quickly that the firefighters were not able to contain them. As the strong wind continued to blow, the fire spread into a blazing wall and roared through dry bushes and trees.

Many eucalyptus trees grew in this area. These trees contain a lot of oil, which is highly flammable. When the flames reached them, the eucalyptus trees exploded, spreading more fire. "When we first got there, trees were blowing up and baseball-sized embers were blowing laterally with the wind—big chunks of them," reported one firefighter.

Those burning chunks fell on the roofs of nearby homes. Many of these homes had wooden shingles for roofs, which caught fire very quickly. By noon, just one hour after the fire was reported, seven hundred houses were burning.

Residents rushed to evacuate their burning neighborhoods. The area's narrow, twisting roads became jammed with cars. As the fire came closer, people were forced to abandon their cars and run for their lives. Some, unfortunately, did not make it. Police officer John Grubensky and five people he tried to rescue were all killed when his patrol car became trapped in the fire.

Animals were on the move too. Residents reported seeing herds of deer along with raccoons, rabbits, and skunks running through their backyards. Many families did not have a chance to rescue family pets, and about one thousand cats and dogs were missing after the fire.

Crews came from all over the area to battle the tremendous fire. By late afternoon, the wind died down and the fire was under control. During that one tragic day, twenty-six people, including many firefighters and police officers, were killed. Three thousand homes were destroyed, and five thousand people were left homeless. Officials estimated the total damages were more than one billion dollars.

Reporter Michael Rogers reported on the eerie scene after the blaze. "With the exception of two chimneys, the neighborhood was completely flat: no decks, no stairways, no second stories. It was still smoldering; the stench of smoke was everywhere."

Slowly, life returned to normal for the victims of the Oakland fire. Homes were rebuilt with tile roofs instead of wood. Dry brush was cut down to prevent future fires, and roads were widened to allow for quicker evacuation and easier access for firefighters.

One of the most notorious disasters in American history did not kill that many people. However, **Hurricane Andrew** caused more monetary damage than any other storm to ever hit the nation and created a scene of unreal destruction.

For many years, experts had been predicting that southern Florida was overdue for a severe hurricane. The first storm of the 1992 hurricane season turned out to be "the big one" that meteorologists were waiting for. Andrew formed in the Atlantic Ocean, became a hurricane on August 22, and was designated Category 5 the following day. Forecasters watched the storm travel toward Florida and urged residents to leave. Hundreds of thousands of people left the area, jamming roads and airports. Thousands more decided to ride out the storm at home.

On August 24, Andrew slammed into **Dade County, Florida**. The storm was so powerful that it destroyed everything in its path. Buildings were ripped apart. Roofs were peeled off houses, and cars, trees, and furniture flew through the air. Andrew's winds were measured at more than 120 mph. The winds were so loud, and one man said that they "sounded like a dozen freight trains on the loose." Heavy rains and a 12-foot-high tidal surge drenched the area.

Families who did not evacuate soon realized they should have left while they could. As windows shattered, roofs flew off, and their houses disintegrated around them, families sought shelter in bathtubs, under mattresses, and in closets. Even people staying in emergency shelters worried that the buildings would collapse on top of them.

When the storm finally passed, it left entire towns in ruins. The town of Homestead, Florida, was especially hard-hit. From horizon to horizon, there was nothing but rubble. Thousands of residents were homeless and had lost everything—their homes, their clothing, their possessions. They did not even have food to eat or water to drink. Victims crowded into tent cities set up by the **Red Cross** and the federal government. These cities had no electricity or phone service, and very little privacy. Residents lined up for donated food and clothing. The **National Guard** came in to prevent looting and keep order.

Many people complained that help was slow in coming. There were not enough shelters or food. Even emergency workers complained that there were not enough materials or volunteers to meet the needs of all the victims. Victims had to wait in long lines to apply for financial aid to rebuild their homes and businesses.

Hurricane Andrew killed twenty-six people and injured hundreds more. More than twenty-five thousand homes were destroyed and two hundred fifty thousand people were left homeless in southern Florida. The storm was the costliest natural disaster in American history until **Hurricane Katrina** in 2005 caused more than $25 billion in damages. It took years for victims to rebuild their lives. As one survivor said, "Andrew changed everyone's outlook as far as what's really important in life."

Heavy snow, high winds, tornadoes, flooding... The storm that struck the East Coast of the United States in March 1993 had just about everything. This amazing weather event became known as the "**Superstorm**" or the "**Storm of the Century**."

In early March, meteorologists sent out a warning that "an enormous storm" would affect much of the **East Coast**. In spite of the warnings, people were stunned by its intensity.

It began snowing at night on Friday, March 12, 1993. Soon, **blizzard** conditions were in effect from New England down to Alabama. Although New England, New York, and other areas of the Northeast are used to heavy snowstorms, the southern states had never seen anything like it. Record snowfalls of twenty inches or more were recorded in Georgia and Tennessee. "In the Southeast, there was more snow than a lot of people had seen in their lifetimes," said Paul Kocin of cable television's The Weather Channel. Mount Mitchell in North Carolina recorded an amazing fifty inches of snow. Heavy winds created snowdrifts up to fourteen feet high in Tennessee and Pennsylvania.

The blizzard was so severe that for the first time in history, every major airport on the East Coast closed. Heavy snow also closed highways all over the east, making travel virtually impossible.

The superstorm was more than just a blizzard. Hurricane-force winds created a powerful **storm surge** that swamped communities along the Gulf Coast of Florida. Sea levels rose six to twelve feet, and streets flooded throughout the area. Eleven **tornadoes** also struck Florida, along with severe thunderstorms. The storm caused millions of dollars in property damage in Florida, making it one of the most expensive non-tropical weather events in the state's history. Another storm surge washed eighteen homes into the ocean in Long Island, New York, and damaged hundreds more from North Carolina to Massachusetts.

The superstorm was followed by several days of high winds and bitter cold temperatures. Records were set all over the country, including 25°F in Pensacola, Florida; 2°F in Birmingham, Alabama; and a wind chill of −40°F in Vermont. Millions lost both heat and electricity as the storm brought down power lines all along the East Coast.

The storm took lives as well. Four people were killed by tornadoes, and eleven died in the storm surge on Florida's Gulf Coast. Others were killed when ships sank in the ocean, and more died in the blizzard, for a total of approximately 270 victims. The storm affected twenty-six states—more than half the country—and caused more than $3 billion in damage. It was truly the "Storm of the Century."

People who live along the **Mississippi River** are used to **flooding**. In 1927, floodwaters rose so high that many residents lost their homes and had to sleep on top of temporary levees built to hold the waters back. Over the next sixty-five years, more floods left the area submerged under water. But the summer of 1993 brought the floodwaters to new heights.

During the spring and summer of 1993, an unusual weather pattern over the **Midwest** produced rain almost every day for three months. Some areas received more than three feet of rain during this period. The enormous amount of rain was too much for the Mississippi River and other rivers in the area, which all overflowed.

Many of the towns along the Mississippi are protected by **levees**, which are walls or ridges intended to regulate water levels and prevent flooding. As the days passed, residents watched the water level climb higher and higher. They piled sandbags on top of the levees to keep the water back, but about seventy percent of the Mississippi's levees failed during the 1993 flood. In some areas, the water rose so high that only the tops of the roofs were visible.

As brown, muddy water flowed into their homes, tens of thousands of residents moved into temporary shelters set up in schools, churches, and municipal buildings. They waited there until the waters receded, and they could go back to see what was left of their homes. Often, they found nothing but smashed furniture, water-soaked walls, warped floors, and several feet of thick, slimy mud. Many homes were also infested with snakes, toads, and frogs.

Other residents refused to leave their homes, in spite of the danger. When the first floors of their houses flooded, owners simply moved upstairs to the second floor. They went in and out of the house by climbing through windows and used boats to travel through the flooded streets.

The 1993 Mississippi River flood was the most destructive flood in United States history. Millions of acres of land were flooded in Illinois, Iowa, Kansas, Minnesota, Missouri, Nebraska, North Dakota, South Dakota, and Wisconsin, and two hundred counties were declared disaster areas by the federal government. Fifty people died.

The flood caused devastating economic damage. Thousands of people lost their jobs when factories and other businesses closed. Barges and other boats that traveled up and down the Mississippi could not operate, and the shipping industry lost an estimated $2 million per day. Floodwaters also washed away crops and destroyed millions of acres of farmland. "Normally, out my front window, I see one hundred acres of corn," said Patty Nelson, a farmer in Clinton, Iowa. "Now these farm fields no longer exist. It's all water." The 1993 flood caused more than $12 billion in property damage.

Even though everyone knows that the Mississippi River will flood again, most residents chose to move back to the area. These people refused to let the river chase them away from their homes.

Disasters often cross national borders. When the ferry **MS Estonia** sank in the frigid waters of the **Baltic Sea**, the loss affected families in Sweden, Estonia, Finland, and other European countries.

The *Estonia* sailed out of **Tallinn, Estonia**, at seven o'clock on the evening of September 27, 1994, bound for Stockholm, Sweden. The ship was crowded with 803 passengers and 186 crew members. In addition, dozens of cars and trucks rode below on the car deck.

Conditions were rough that night, with heavy rain and strong winds causing very high waves. The poor conditions created an uncomfortable ride. Despite the rough seas, the ship was moving rather fast in order to stay on schedule and dock in Stockholm by 9:30 a.m. the next morning.

Just after one o'clock in the morning, though, as the ship neared the Finnish island of Uto, passengers heard a strange thump. A wave had jolted open the bow door, where cars had been driven onto the ship. Water flowed into the car deck, and the ship began to sink.

"Suddenly the table and the suitcases tumbled down in the cabin," recalled one survivor. Another, who had been in the ship's bar, described it as: "The cozy atmosphere in the bar with people singing, laughing, and having a good time was just in a few seconds to be changed to total chaos. Suddenly the ship leaned down on the side... A crowd of people fell to the wall, breaking arms and legs."

By the time an alarm sounded through the ship, it was too late for most of the passengers to escape. Fewer than two hundred people managed to escape from the *Estonia* before it sank. As they floated in the 50°F water or clung to pieces of debris, many drowned or died from **hypothermia**, which is the state of having dangerously low body heat. When rescue ships and helicopters reached the area, they found only 137 people alive. Doctors said it was a miracle that anyone had survived at all.

However, 852 people did not make it, and many bodies of the dead were never recovered. It was Europe's worst maritime disaster since World War II had ended more than fifty years prior.

Although the manufacturer and operator of the *Estonia* denied that there were any problems, a joint Swedish-Finnish investigation into the disaster soon found that the cause was a faulty cargo door. Because of a design flaw, the ship's cargo door was not strong enough to hold back the rough waves. However, these findings have also been widely disputed.

Swedish safety inspectors also reported that they had told the crew that the cargo doors "didn't look good" before the ship left. However, the inspectors were not making an official visit at the time, so the crew disregarded their warning. Investigators also said the crew should have slowed or stopped the ship once the broken cargo door was discovered. This series of mistakes cost the lives of more than 850 people, including many of the crew members who had ignored the warnings.

Japan is often struck by **earthquakes**, and for many years, the nation's government prided itself on its strict building codes and disaster readiness. However, when a major earthquake struck the crowded city of **Kobe** on January 17, 1995, Japan's disaster preparations were put to the test—and failed miserably.

Kobe is a port city in western Japan. At the time, the city had a population of almost 1.5 million people. Most residents were sleeping when a 7.2-magnitude earthquake struck the city at 5:46 a.m. The quake was the most powerful in Japan since 1923.

The earthquake was so strong that it knocked trains off their tracks, collapsed elevated highways and bridges, and destroyed thousands of buildings. Terrified residents ran into the streets, some wrapped in blankets and sheets they had pulled hastily from their beds. Thousands more were trapped in collapsed buildings and were unable to escape. The central part of Kobe, which included the city's docks and port area, suffered the most damage. This area had been built on soft rock and earth. The earthquake liquefied the ground here, causing buildings to collapse and huge cranes in the harbor to fall over.

The earthquake was just the beginning of the misery for the city's residents. Powerful aftershocks also struck the area, and huge fires burned out of control throughout the city. An estimated five hundred people died in these blazes. Electricity, natural gas service, phone service, and water was cut off to millions of people.

Although Japan had prided itself on how efficiently it could respond to a disaster, it soon became clear that officials did not have an organized plan to help victims. Several days after the quake, residents left without homes were still camped out on the streets or living in unheated shelters. There was not enough food or water. Relief supplies could not get into the area because roads were blocked by rubble from collapsed highways and bridges. When Japanese Prime Minister **Tomichi Murayama** was criticized, he admitted that the early response had been "confused" and that the nation had to "rethink and restructure our disaster relief policies."

The devastation of the Kobe earthquake also took engineers by surprise. Many buildings in the area were new and had been built to strict codes that were supposed to prevent collapse. However, these buildings did not stand up to the quake. In addition, bridges that were supposed to be earthquake-proof also collapsed. One section of collapsed roadway was almost half a mile long.

"The situation is terrible and it's going to get worse," said one Japanese soldier who was helping with the rescue effort. He was right. More than fifty-five hundred people were killed and thirty-seven thousand were injured in the quake. Damage was estimated at $100 billion. The Kobe earthquake was a brutal reminder of how difficult it really is to be prepared for a terrible disaster.

Oklahoma City, Oklahoma, seemed like a safe area in April 1995. The city was located in the heartland of America—a place where it did not seem likely that anything terrible could ever happen. But that all changed on Wednesday, April 19, 1995.

The nine-story **Alfred P. Murrah Federal Building** in downtown Oklahoma City was a busy place that morning. Federal employees worked, customers waited in line for various government offices, and children played happily in the America's Kids daycare center on the second floor.

Shortly before 9:00 a.m., a yellow Ryder truck pulled up in front of the building. At 9:02 a.m., a two-ton bomb inside the truck exploded. The blast ripped off the front of the Murrah Building. The explosion could be seen, heard, and felt as far as thirty miles away.

Rescue workers and ordinary citizens rushed to the scene and began digging at the huge pile of rubble, looking for survivors. Heavy equipment was brought in to remove large pieces of debris. Specially trained teams of search-and-rescue dogs joined as well.

Many of those killed in the explosion were children. Only six children in the day-care center survived the blast. Many were seriously injured, suffering severe burns, brain damage, and broken bones. Other children were killed because they were in the building with parents or grandparents.

Daycare center victim Baylee Almon had just celebrated her first birthday the day before the disaster. A photograph of a fire-fighter gently carrying her lifeless body out of the wreckage became a heartbreaking symbol of the disaster.

Around one o'clock in the morning on April 20, the last survivor—a 15-year-old girl—was pulled from the rubble. The disaster had claimed 168 lives and injured eight hundred others.

Americans were stunned by the bombing and reached out to help in any way they could. Hundreds of people lined up to donate blood for the injured victims. Oklahoma restaurants donated more than one hundred twenty thousand meals to rescue workers and other volunteers, and the **Salvation Army** donated one hundred thousand more. About one thousand emergency workers from all over the country took part in the rescue.

Investigators knew right away that a bomb was to blame for the disaster. A few days later, the **Federal Bureau of Investigation (FBI)** arrested 27-year-old Timothy McVeigh. McVeigh was a member of several right-wing militia groups that believed the American government was working against the people. He planned the Oklahoma City bombing for April 19, the second anniversary of the government's raid on a cult called the **Branch Davidians**.

McVeigh was convicted of murder and sentenced to death by lethal injection. On June 11, 2001, he was executed at a federal prison. His accomplice, **Terry Nichols**, was also convicted and sentenced to life in prison.

The remains of the Murrah Federal Building were torn down shortly after the bombing. Today, the area is a park with a monument for the 168 victims—an eerie reminder of the tragedy that took place.

Disasters can happen anywhere, and often rough conditions can make rescue and recovery efforts extremely difficult. Emergency workers who rushed to the scene of a **plane crash** in **Florida** faced terrain that made it almost impossible for them to do their jobs.

ValuJet was a budget airline that flew between cities in Florida and other destinations in the American South. The airline had only been in business since 1993, but in that short time, it had suffered a number of problems including rough landings and a fire. However, travelers enjoyed the no-frills airline's low fares, and the airline continued to operate.

On May 11, 1996, ValuJet Flight 592 took off from Miami International Airport on a trip to Atlanta. Just eight minutes after takeoff, the pilot reported smoke in the cockpit. Then, the plane disappeared from the radar screen and crashed into the swampy waters of the Florida Everglades.

The pilot of a small plane who saw the crash reported that the plane had hit the ground at such a steep angle that "nothing could have survived. The wreckage looked like someone took garbage and threw it on the ground."

Rescuers who rushed to the site faced many challenges. The plane had crashed into water that was four to five feet deep. The water was so dark and muddy that divers could not see anything. The area was also filled with sawgrass, a type of plant with razor-sharp leaves that made it impossible

Memorial near the crash site, dedicated to the one hundred ten victims

to walk through. In addition, the swampy waters were home to alligators.

Despite the difficult conditions, emergency workers continued to search. However, it soon became clear that all 110 people on board the plane had died. For months afterward, the victims' personal belongings—including credit cards, clothing, and wallets—floated to the surface, where they were gathered up by detectives investigating the crash.

As usual after a plane crash, the **NTSB** held hearings to discover the cause. After almost a year, the Board declared that a fire had started in the cargo hold and filled the cabin and cockpit with smoke. It had probably been caused by several oxygen canisters. Oxygen is highly flammable and considered hazardous cargo. The canisters on the plane were labeled as empty, but they did have oxygen in them, which exploded and caused the fire.

The ValuJet crash led to stricter rules about carrying hazardous cargo. In addition, the **Federal Aviation Administration (FAA)** demanded that planes carry fire detectors and extinguishers in their cargo holds.

After the crash, the FAA grounded ValuJet because of safety violations. However, in late September 1996, ValuJet received permission to fly again. Soon afterward, the airline changed its name to **AirTran**, and continued to operate as a budget airline until it was acquired by **Southwest Airlines** in 2011.

On a warm summer night near New York City, many people were enjoying the evening on boats in the ocean. Others were on the beaches that stretch across **Long Island's** southern shore. Suddenly, fire in the sky shattered the peaceful evening. As people watched in shock and horror, pieces of an airplane crashed into the water. The doomed plane was **Flight 800**, a **Boeing 747** headed from New York to Paris, France.

Until the explosion, everything had been normal on Trans World Airlines (TWA) Flight 800, which carried 212 passengers and eighteen crew members. The plane took off shortly after eight o'clock in the evening. Around 8:30 p.m., without warning, the plane exploded.

The back of the plane, which included most of the passenger cabin, fell toward the ocean at a high speed. The front continued flying for a few seconds before it too plunged down. One of the fuel tanks burst open from the tremendous force of the wind pushing against the plane. Then the front of the plane exploded and hit the water.

Many people along the shore got into their boats and rushed to the site to look for survivors. A Coast Guard ship also joined the search. But none of the two hundred thirty people aboard TWA Flight 800 had survived the explosion or the impact of smashing into the ocean.

The explosion of Flight 800 devastated families around the United States, France, and several other countries. The small town of Montoursville, Pennsylvania, lost sixteen members of the high school's French club, their teacher, and four other adults, who were on their way to Paris for an educational trip.

Finding and identifying the bodies was not easy. Many had been torn to pieces by the force of the crash. Others were still inside the plane when it sank to the bottom of the Atlantic Ocean and could not be recovered for several weeks. Other bodies washed up on beaches and were found by passersby.

Specially trained divers gathered the remains of the plane, which were scattered over five miles of ocean. The pieces were brought to an airplane hangar on Long Island, where the plane was put back together and studied. Experts also analyzed the plane's cockpit voice recorder and flight data recorder. They revealed that everything had been working fine before the explosion.

Many people were sure that a bomb or a missile had blown up the plane. However, no traces of explosives were found. After investigating the crash for sixteen months, the **FBI** and the **NTSB** announced that Flight 800 had exploded due to a mechanical failure. The empty center fuel tank on the plane held vapors of highly explosive jet fuel. A spark, possibly from some worn-out wires in the tank, had ignited those vapors and caused a powerful explosion.

Over the years, families and friends of the victims have returned to the site on the anniversary of the crash to toss flowers into the water. The crash of Flight 800 affected lives all over the world.

In some parts of the world, floods are a way of life. Many areas of **China** experience a summer **rainy season** that floods major rivers. However, even these expected floods can sometimes get out of hand, as millions of Chinese people discovered during the summer of 1998.

In 1998, China's rainy season arrived almost a month early. Unusually heavy rains during the spring, combined with an early snowmelt, led to an emergency situation by the middle of July.

The **Yangtze River** in central China was especially hard-hit. In some areas, the river's water level rose so fast that residents had little chance to gather their possessions and escape. More than fourteen million people were forced to leave their homes, and more than six million homes were destroyed.

With their homes leveled and their villages washed away, millions of residents moved onto the tops of levees and built small shelters out of straw and plastic bags. Medical experts and government officials worried that diseases would spread quickly through these makeshift communities, which lacked clean water and food.

The flooding also destroyed approximately eleven million acres of farmland. Most of the summer rice crop was destroyed, causing severe shortages in a country that often faced trouble feeding its burgeoning population.

As floodwaters ravaged cities and villages, the Chinese government asked citizens to do everything possible to strengthen levees and try to hold the river back. Residents piled sandbags along roadways and in front of their homes and businesses. Almost a million soldiers from the Chinese army rushed to help rebuild levees and help citizens.

For centuries, the Chinese government has avoided alerting the world about trouble or disasters within its borders. However, the 1998 floods were too much to handle independently. The Chinese government asked the world for assistance, and food, money, medical equipment, and other aid poured in from countries around the globe. The **Red Cross** and other international aid organizations also came to China.

The estimated death toll for the 1998 floods was approximately four thousand people, although the actual total may have been higher. While the Chinese government blamed heavy rainfall and other bad weather for the floods, many experts agreed that people were also responsible for much of the damage. People have settled in flood-prone areas that used to be uninhabited, which puts more residents in danger of flooding and prevents rivers from safely overflowing their banks. However, China has such a huge population—approximately 1.4 billion people—that there is tremendous pressure to utilize every piece of land.

In addition, many of the forests along the banks of the Yangtze and other rivers have been cut down. This causes heavy rains to wash away soil and dump it into the rivers, raising water levels and causing more flooding. The combination of human changes and natural events has led to disaster time and time again.

The residents of the small fishing community of Peggy's Cove, Nova Scotia, Canada, were used to tragedies at sea. However, on the night of September 2, disaster struck the village in a completely different form.

Swissair Flight 111 had left John F. Kennedy International Airport in Long Island, New York, at 8:18 p.m. that evening on a non-stop flight to Geneva, Switzerland. About an hour later, while passengers were sleeping or enjoying in-flight entertainment, the cockpit of the plane filled with smoke. The pilot asked air traffic controllers for permission to make an emergency landing in Boston, but the controllers told him to head for Halifax, Nova Scotia, because that airport was closer.

About half an hour later, the **Boeing MD-11** aircraft reached the coast of Nova Scotia. The pilot told air traffic control that he would dump some fuel into the Atlantic Ocean to prepare for an emergency landing at Halifax, only seven miles away. The plane descended to somewhere between eight thousand to ten thousand feet—and then it disappeared from the radar.

At the same time, villagers in Peggy's Cove saw a flash of light and heard an explosion. Swissair Flight 111 had crashed into the Atlantic Ocean.

Many of Peggy's Cove's residents owned boats, and they quickly sailed to the crash site to rescue survivors. But all they found were bodies and pieces of plane. All 215 passengers and fourteen crew members had been killed. More than half of the victims—137 people—were Americans. Seven members of the United Nations staff and a pioneer in AIDS research were among the dead.

Over the next few days, tiny Peggy's Cove became the headquarters for an international recovery effort. The Royal Canadian Mounted Police, the Canadian Coast Guard, and specially trained divers from the Canadian Navy faced the grim task of recovering bodies. The recovery effort was called **Operation: Perseverance** and covered miles of beaches and ocean. Villagers also aided in the recovery efforts, although they were deeply upset by the tragedy.

Investigators soon decided that faulty wiring on the plane had caused the smoke and subsequent fire that led to the crash. An official with the **Canadian Transportation Safety Board** reported heat discoloration in the ceiling panels that was caused by overheated light bulbs. The wiring for the in-flight entertainment system also may have been at fault, although many investigators admit that they will never know the exact cause of the crash for certain.

After the crash, investigators recommended that all MD-11 aircraft be inspected for wiring problems. The disaster led to improved electrical systems, as well as the replacement of insulation material that may have been fuel for the fire. Like so many other disasters, the tragedy of Swissair Flight 111 may save thousands of other lives around the world in years to come.

Any natural disaster can cause tremendous damage and suffering. When the victims are desperately poor, however, the devastation caused by a storm or an earthquake turns into an even greater tragedy.

On October 21, 1998, meteorologists got their first look at the storm that would soon become **Hurricane Mitch,** when they spotted a tropical depression forming in the southern **Caribbean Sea**. The next day, the storm was officially declared a

tropical depression, and on October 23, it strengthened into one of the most powerful Atlantic storms to hit the region.

Mitch was a slow-moving storm, and the longer it remained over water, the more powerful it became. By the morning of October 28, the storm had stalled just north of **Honduras** in Central America. Heavy rain inundated the country along with the neighboring nation of **Nicaragua**. The rain caused widespread flooding and mudslides.

Many of the residents of Honduras and Nicaragua are destitute and live in precariously built houses. These fragile homes were no match for the driving rain, and they were swept away by the storm. Thousands of victims drowned as their homes collapsed. Many victims took refuge in trees, only to lose their lives as those also washed away in the floodwaters.

People who sought shelter in sturdier buildings did not fare much better. In Morolica, Honduras, the water destroyed a school being used as an evacuation center, forcing parents to grab sleeping babies and children out of the water's deadly path.

Nicaragua also suffered severe damage. At least one thousand people were killed in a mudslide near the Casita volcano. Others drowned when Lake Managua overflowed its banks and linked with Lake Nicaragua.

After battering the Caribbean, Mitch finally moved north toward Florida. By then, the storm had lost most of its punch, and it was quickly downgraded to a tropical storm. However, the devastation it left behind was almost unbelievable. Officials estimated that up to eighteen thousand people died in the disaster, including sixteen thousand in Honduras alone. One BBC reporter described the country as being "in a state of profound shock." Honduran **President Carlos Flores** said, "We have before us a panorama of death, desolation, and ruin in all the national territory."

Mitch's devastation went far beyond the high death toll. The storm left about six hundred thousand people homeless and destroyed roads and bridges across Honduras and Nicaragua. Almost all crops were also destroyed, further damaging the economy. Because Honduras and Nicaragua were already economically weak countries, most of this damage could not be repaired. Both countries appealed to other nations for help immediately after the disaster and in the months that followed.

The *City of New Orleans* passenger train became well-known in a popular song by Arlo Guthrie during the 1960s. Years later, **Amtrak** named its Chicago–New Orleans train after its famous predecessor. On March 15, 1999, however, the train became famous for a much different and deadlier reason.

When the Amtrak train left Chicago that Monday night, it was loaded with 216 passengers and crew. Many were settled in for the night in a sleeper car behind the two engines at the front of the train. At 9:45 p.m., the train approached a road crossing in Bourbonnais, a town of about fourteen thousand people just fifty miles south of Chicago. As the engineer approached the crossing, he was horrified to see a truck crossing the tracks.

John Stokes was driving a tractor trailer loaded with steel rails. Although warning lights and gates at the crossing should have prevented him from crossing the tracks, Stokes claimed that they did not come on until after he was already on top of the tracks. By then, it was too late to avoid disaster. The train smashed into the tractor trailer and derailed. One of the engines hit the car behind it, then split open, setting off an explosion and fire.

"All of a sudden, everything just started crashing and catching on fire and people were hollering and running," said one passenger. Another reported, "It was pitch-dark. Our eyes had to adjust... I didn't know whether I was going to get out, or if it would explode."

Rescuers rushed to the scene. One eyewitness said that the derailed train looked like an accordion, and the air was "split with screaming and moaning." Eleven of the train's fourteen cars had derailed, along with both engines. Rescuers, some using specially trained dogs, faced the grim task of searching each car for victims. Once a car was searched, it was spray-painted "empty" to alert other workers.

More than one hundred passengers were injured in the crash, and eleven were killed. All the dead had been riding in the sleeper car.

The investigation into the accident focused on the gates and warning lights at the road crossing. At first, many people blamed the truck driver, John Stokes, insisting that he must have tried to beat the train across the tracks. Stokes also came under suspicion because he had a poor driving record and was on probation at the time of the crash. Stokes insisted that the crossing gates were up when he started across the tracks, and parked train cars near the crossing blocked his view of the oncoming train.

Extensive testing of the signals at the crossing showed they were not actually working properly. Prosecutors had intended to charge Stokes with involuntary manslaughter, but they changed their minds after learning about the malfunctioning safety equipment. Instead, Stokes was charged with violating hours of service regulations since he had been driving for thirty hours straight at the time of the crash. Railroad officials set up new inspection plans for crossing signals to prevent future accidents.

The French town of **Chamonix** was already experiencing a rough winter by early 1999. On February 9, an avalanche killed twelve people, and six days later, a fire burned down the center of town. But something worse yet would befall the village in the Alps just six weeks later.

On the morning of March 24, 1999, a Belgian truck was traveling through the seven-mile-long **Mont Blanc tunnel** that ran through an Alpine mountain and connected Chamonix to Courmayeur, Italy. At 11:00 a.m., the truck caught fire in the middle of the tunnel. The blaze raged on, trapping dozens of people and destroying at least twenty trucks and eleven cars.

Fighting the fire was especially difficult because of its location deep inside the mountain. Fuel from trapped cars and trucks fed the inferno, raising temperatures to more than 1,800°F. Parts of the road's surface melted from the heat, and a section of the ceiling collapsed, making rescue efforts even more difficult. Firefighters could only enter the tunnel from the Italian side because toxic fumes and smoke were pouring out of the French entrance. It took two days to put out the flames. By then, thirty-nine people were dead.

The Mont Blanc tunnel had opened in 1965, and by 1999, approximately seven hundred fifty thousand trucks traveled over it annually. Although the 1999 accident was the first fatal fire in the tunnel, residents of the area had been complaining about safety conditions for years. They worried about large, heavy trucks navigating the narrow, winding mountains roads that were never designed for truck traffic.

The accident also focused attention on the danger of serious accidents or fires inside the tunnel. Although the Mont Blanc tunnel was equipped with heat-resistant shelters, a smoke filtration system, and an emergency broadcast system that issued warnings to motorists, none of these had been enough to prevent the catastrophe of March 24. "Fate's got nothing to do with it," said Chamonix's mayor, Michel Carlet. "We've always been afraid of something like this."

After the disaster, the **French Transport Ministry** quickly began an investigation. A spokesperson said that the accident had "shown that fires can break out in tunnels of a power we'd never imagined up to now." Still, there had been indications that something tragic could happen. A year before the disaster, a report from the area's fire and rescue departments found fault with emergency procedures and complained that emergency drills had never been held.

For three years after the accident, the Mont Blanc tunnel was closed to all traffic as workers rebuilt the structure and officials decided how to make it safer. In March 2002, cars were allowed to pass through it again, with small trucks and buses following in April. It was not until May 2002, though, that Mont Blanc opened again to large trucks. The return of the tractor trailers caused a protest by environmentalists and safety advocates, but they could do nothing to stop the return of heavy trucks through the dangerous mountain pass.

Some countries are no strangers to **earthquakes**. But even in these tremor-prone nations, the destruction and loss of life in a major earthquake can be almost beyond belief.

İzmit, an industrial town in northwestern **Turkey**, was quiet at 3:02 a.m. on the morning of August 17. Suddenly, part of a major fault line shifted, causing an earthquake that measured 7.4 on the Richter scale. Most residents of İzmit and the surrounding cities were sleeping when the quake struck and had no chance to escape.

Many buildings in the area were poorly constructed, and they collapsed like a house of cards during the powerful quake. Thousands of people were killed instantly as their houses collapsed on top of them. Many more were trapped in the rubble and died of injuries or dehydration before they could be rescued. Many areas were destroyed by fires, which were ignited when gas from leaking lines and damaged oil refineries lighted.

In all, more than seventeen thousand people died. In just one city, **Golcuk**, five thousand people died. As many as a million others camped outside or in tents because they were afraid to return to their damaged homes or had no homes to return to. A young boy, who was rescued after spending eighty hours underneath the rubble, was the only bright spot in the recovery effort.

Many people criticized the government for its slow and inefficient response after the earthquake. A government spokesman defended the response, saying: "The magnitude of the disaster is beyond all comprehension. This is beyond the capability of any government in the world." Still, the lack of equipment and trained rescue personnel made many citizens resort to digging through the rubble with shovels or with their bare hands in a desperate effort to free trapped relatives. "If there was a military official or another high-level person lying here, they would have rescue teams. But here, we are only citizens, digging alone," complained one man.

The government was also criticized for allowing unsafe housing to be built. Crowds held rallies and shouted protests such as "Government, resign!" Although many residents demanded that officials be arrested, little was done to assign responsibility.

Although Turkey's government did send some aid to stricken areas, most help came from aid societies such as the **Red Cross** and the **Turkish Red Crescent**. Experts estimated the total damage to have been between $3 billion and $8 billion. In addition to the lost homes and businesses, residents had to face the loss of family members and friends, as well as horrifying memories of the disaster. Months and years after the disaster, aid workers reported treating residents for post-traumatic stress disorder (PTSD) and were still trying to find permanent housing for thousands of people still living in tent cities.

◆ Traveling at supersonic speeds on a luxury plane called the **Concorde** was comfortable, fast, and efficient. It was also extremely safe—until disaster struck in 2000.

Only two airlines, **British Airways** and **Air France**, had Concordes. These specially designed planes traveled up to 1,350 mph, which is faster than the speed of sound. These supersonic speeds allowed the planes to cross the Atlantic in less than four hours—almost half the time of a regular flight. Tickets cost at least $9,000, but passengers received first-class service as well as a quick flight. The Concorde's safety record was almost perfect. The only serious accident had occurred in 1979, when a tire blew out on a rough landing.

Air France Flight 4590 took off from Charles de Gaulle Airport in Paris shortly before five o'clock. The luxury airplane had 109 people on board. As the plane took off, something went terribly wrong. A Federal Express pilot named Sid Hare was in the area and saw the crash. "The airplane was struggling to climb and obviously couldn't get altitude," Hare reported. As the plane rose about two hundred feet, flames began streaming from an engine on the left side of the plane. "The airplane stalled, the nose went straight up into the air, and the airplane actually rolled over to the left and almost inverted when it went down in a huge fireball. It was a sickening sight—a huge fireball."

The Concorde crashed into a hotel in Gonesse, a town just outside of Paris. All 109 people on board were killed, and so were four others in the hotel. It was the first deadly crash in the Concorde's twenty-three-year history.

An investigation began immediately after the crash. At first, inspectors focused on the plane's wings, because British Airways had recently reported cracks in their Concordes' wings. However, investigators quickly decided that the wings were not at fault in the Paris tragedy. Instead, the problem was on the ground.

On August 10, 2001, just over a year after the crash, France released the investigation's official report. It said that a strip of metal had fallen from a Continental airplane that had taken off from the same runway earlier that day. The Concorde had hit the metal, which had punctured the supersonic plane's tire. Strips of rubber and metal had flown back into the Concorde's fuel tank, causing a gas leak and a fire that destroyed the plane.

As a result of the accident, maintenance procedures at the airport were changed. A few months later, in November 2001, Air France's Concorde took to the skies once again. Officials hoped that the plane's safety record would continue to be the best in the industry, but due to a slump in air travel after the Air France crash and the September 11 attacks, Air France and British Airways retired the Concorde in 2003.

Confusion can surround any disaster. But when the tragedy involves a military submarine and a publicity-shy government, finding out what really happened can be even more complicated than usual.

On August 12, 2000, two powerful explosions ripped through the Russian submarine **Kursk** as it began a series of torpedo-firing tests in the **Barents Sea**. Nearby ships, as well as a seismic monitoring device on shore 279 miles away, recorded the blasts. The crippled submarine sank to the bottom of the sea, carrying 118 crewmen with it.

At first, Russia claimed that the submarine had collided with another submarine, perhaps another American submarine stationed nearby. Another theory was that the submarine had struck an unexploded mine that had been left in the sea after World War II. It was not until much later that the Russian government admitted that the submarine had exploded because of a malfunction on board the ship.

While the governments argued, rescuers tried to figure out how to raise the damaged ship. Tapping sounds led rescue crews to believe that there were survivors on board the submarine, but later it was announced that these sounds had come from mechanical devices and not human beings. Russia insisted that everyone on board had died instantly.

At first, Russia refused foreign aid to raise the submarine, but after a week of fruitless efforts, it finally accepted help from international experts. By then, there was no hope of finding any survivors. When Norwegian divers finally reached the submarine, they found it to be flooded. The front part of the ship, which included the torpedo room, the command center, the radio room, and the living quarters, were completely destroyed.

The *Kursk* remained on the bottom of the Barents Sea for two and a half months. Finally, in late October, divers reached the ship and managed to climb inside. Bodies found in the front part of the ship showed evidence of having been killed instantly by the explosions.

However, twenty-three more bodies were found in the rear compartment of the submarine. One of them was 27-year-old Lieutenant-Captain **Dmitri Kolesnikov**, the commander of the ship. Kolesnikov had written a note describing the sailors' ordeal. He described how the twenty-three men sought refuge in the rear compartment, even though they knew there was no chance of escape or rescue. Then he wrapped the note in plastic and placed it in his pocket.

Almost two years after the accident, the Russian government issued an official report about the *Kursk* disaster. The report stated that the ship had exploded when hydrogen peroxide, used as torpedo fuel, leaked out of its compartment and ignited. The second explosion was caused when the fire reached ammunition stored on the ship. The announcement was embarrassing for Russia, whose military fleet had deteriorated badly over the past ten years, but families of the victims were comforted that the truth about the accident had finally come out.

On the morning of September 11, 2001, an unprecedented terrorist attack on America changed the way the country—and world—saw itself.

That morning, thousands of people made their way to the **World Trade Center** in the Financial District of Lower Manhattan. This complex of seven buildings included two 110-story towers, the tallest buildings in the city.

At 8:46 a.m., hijacked **American Airlines Flight 11** flew into the North Tower of the World Trade Center, setting off a tremendous explosion and fire. Seventeen minutes later, **United Airlines Flight 175**, which had also been hijacked after leaving Boston, crashed into the South Tower.

Firefighters and police officers rushed to the scene and rescued hundreds. As survivors straggled out of the buildings after walking down dozens of flights of stairs, they dodged large falling pieces of concrete and metal, along with the bodies of desperate people who had jumped from the upper floors to their deaths.

The fires melted the steel support columns in both towers. At 10:05 a.m., the South Tower collapsed. At 10:28 a.m., the North Tower followed, imploding into a pile of twisted metal and smashed concrete. Thousands were killed instantly including 343 firefighters. It was, by far, the largest loss of life in the New York City Fire Department's history.

The Twin Towers were now a pile of twisted steel, concrete, and other debris that stood more than ten stories high. It soon became clear that almost no one had survived. The final death toll was 2,819. Fewer than half of the victims were recovered because their bodies were vaporized by the force of the collapsing concrete and the tremendous heat of the fires.

The World Trade Center was not the only target that morning. At 9:43 a.m., the **Pentagon** in Washington, DC, was struck by hijacked **American Airlines Flight 77**, causing a fire and partial building collapse that killed approximately two hundred people. Another plane, **United Airlines Flight 93**, had been hijacked after it left Newark Liberty International Airport in New Jersey, and was probably headed for the White House or the U.S. Capitol building. However, passengers fought back against the hijackers, causing the plane to crash in a field near **Shanksville, Pennsylvania**, killing everyone on board.

The World Trade Center had been targeted by terrorists before. In 1993, a truck bomb detonated in the parking garage below the North Tower and killed six. That attack was organized by **Islamic extremists**, and the same was true of the September 11 attacks. Within hours, the FBI blamed **Osama bin Laden**, the leader of Islamic militant organization **al-Qaeda**, and who lived in Afghanistan. A few weeks later, the United States and allies began a decades-long war to eliminate terrorist threats in that country.

For a few days after the attacks, normal life stopped. But despite the national trauma, Americans were proud of their country. Flags flew from businesses, houses, and cars, and patriotic songs were sung at public gatherings. Police officers, firefighters, and rescue workers became heroes. The country demonstrated that sometimes tragedy can bring about tremendous good and unity.

New York City was still reeling from the terrorist attacks of September 11 when death and destruction came from the skies once again.

It was November 12, 2001, Veterans Day, and many residents of New York City's borough of **Queens** were enjoying a day off from school and work. Two months prior, the city's peace had been shattered by a terrorist attack that destroyed the World Trade Center, killing more than twenty-eight hundred people. The neighborhood of **Belle Harbor**, Queens, and surrounding communities, had been especially hard-hit, losing more than ninety residents that day. However, residents were once again tuning out the sound of low-flying planes taking off from nearby John F. Kennedy International Airport (JFK).

At 9:14 a.m. that morning, **American Airlines Flight 587** left JFK, heading toward the Dominican Republic. Although the take-off seemed normal, something went terribly wrong just minutes later. Witnesses saw parts of the plane fall off as it passed over Belle Harbor. Then, at 9:17 a.m., the plane crashed into houses below. One of the engines landed on a gas station, while another fell onto a boat parked in a driveway.

Within seconds, several streets in Belle Harbor were a blazing inferno. Firefighters and other rescuers rushed to the scene. "Hollywood couldn't have dreamed up something like this," said one firefighter as he surveyed the destruction.

Meanwhile, New York City Mayor Rudy Giuliani put the city on high alert. Until proof came that this was not another terrorist attack, all airports and most bridges were closed.

The crash killed all 260 people on board. It also claimed the lives of five people on the ground, who had been killed when pieces of the plane crashed into their houses and started fires. The disaster was the second-deadliest airplane crash in United States history.

The **NTSB** began an immediate investigation of the crash. It soon determined that the crash was an accident and not a terrorist act. The Board investigated several possible causes, but discovered that, according to flight records, Flight 587 had taken off less than two minutes after the plane in front of it had left the ground. The first plane's take-off created powerful air turbulence that caused the first officer of Flight 587 to move the plane's rudders repeatedly and aggressively. These actions caused the vertical stabilizer (the fin on the tail of the plane) to break off due to the wind. This also caused the pilots to lose control of the plane. These findings caused American Airlines to modify its pilot training program to prevent similar errors in the future.

It only takes a second for merrymaking to turn into disaster. Even holiday celebrations can turn disastrous, as happened in the crowded streets of **Lima, Peru**, in 2001.

Saturday, December 29, was a busy shopping day in Lima. Crowds of people packed the **Mesa Redonda** shopping district—made mostly of wood and adobe buildings along narrow streets—buying food and party supplies for the upcoming New Year's holiday. One of the most popular items for sale were fireworks, which were legal to sell and use in the South American country.

Suddenly, the joyful scene turned tragic. A vendor, either on the street or inside a crowded store, lit a firework to demonstrate how it worked. The explosion started a fire that immediately roared out of control. Within minutes, four blocks of shops and apartment buildings were ablaze.

The throngs of people in the street and inside the packed buildings had little chance of escaping the inferno. "At first it was like an earthquake with a horrible noise—there were lights everywhere and a giant explosion," said one eyewitness. Fed by the highly flammable materials inside the shops, including paint, paper, and clothing, the fire raged out of control for hours, despite the best efforts of hundreds of firefighters. The fire's extremely high temperatures—perhaps more than 1,100°F—and a shortage of water made the job even more difficult. Several firefighters, including the city's fire chief, said the fire was the worst they had ever seen.

When the fire was finally extinguished several hours later, rescuers faced a horrible scene. The streets and stores were littered with charred bodies. Some were burned to the bone, while others were little more than unrecognizable, blackened lumps. Many of the bodies were of children who had been enjoying an outing with their families. At least 282 people were killed, and more than one hundred more were injured. Peruvian Health Minister Luis Solari said that some bodies would never be found because the tremendous heat of the fire had destroyed them.

Recovery efforts were made even more difficult by the piles of wreckage as well as fears that some of the damaged buildings might collapse. In addition, many shop owners locked their doors behind them as they fled. They did this to prevent looting, but their actions slowed rescue and recovery efforts.

Shortly after the blaze, **President Alejandro Toledo** announced that he would ban the production and sale of fireworks. However, despite the disaster that brought 2001 to a tragic close, fireworks remain a popular part of Peruvian celebrations—a tradition that seems likely to continue in the future.

Sometimes a disaster can cause one terrible incident after another, like a row of dominoes. That is exactly what happened in the **Democratic Republic of the Congo (the Congo)** in early 2002.

The Central African country of the Congo is one of the poorest countries in the world, and living conditions there are abysmal for many, even at the best of times. The area suffers from chronic water shortages and has also been caught in the middle of deadly warfare.

In mid-January 2002, another disaster struck the area when **Mount Nyiragongo**, one of the most active volcanoes in Africa, began erupting. Rivers of lava up to 160 feet wide and ten feet deep swept through the city of Goma. Almost half the city was destroyed, including at least ten thousand homes, a Roman Catholic cathedral, and part of the runway at the city's airport. "Goma has been split completely in half, and one half is totally destroyed," reported Stephen Johnson, a humanitarian affairs officer with the United Nations.

A huge river of molten lava poured into Lake Kivu. The lava created a huge cloud of steam and threatened to ignite methane gas from the lake.

The eruption and burning lava killed approximately forty people. Almost five hundred thousand more were left homeless by the destruction, which created an entirely new kind of disaster. Hundreds of thousands of refugees streamed out of the area. Some traveled to other parts of the Congo, while most crossed over the eastern border and entered the country of Rwanda. Families were separated as they rushed to escape, and reporters told of waves of exhausted people carrying mattresses and cooking pots.

Other residents were trapped in Goma by the advancing lava and were left with no shelter or supplies. "There is no food, no water, no sanitation. We are here like animals," said one man who barely escaped the city.

The **United Nations** and other organizations sent food and relief supplies to the area. However, reaching Goma was difficult because lava had cut off roads and closed the airport, so everything had to be delivered by boat. Meanwhile, aid workers worried that disease would spread because of the poor living conditions.

As the days passed, many residents returned to Goma, even though conditions there were hardly fit for living. People scavenged for food and building supplies in the lava flows and in abandoned homes and businesses. Then another tragedy struck. Lava ignited fumes from a gas station and created a tremendous explosion and fire. Another series of explosions occurred when a dozen 50-gallon barrels of fuel in a storeroom exploded, sending flames one hundred feet into the air. At least thirty people who were scooping fuel into plastic containers at the station were killed.

A few days later, the fires burned out, and Mount Nyiragongo was quiet once again. Life went back to normal in Goma, although the disaster made "normal" more difficult than ever.

◆ Can a train catch fire and burn without the crew knowing? Tragically, this is what happened when disaster struck near Cairo, Egypt, in a city called **El Ayyat**.

On February 20, 2002, almost four hundred people were crammed onto a train traveling from Cairo to Luxor. The train had been designed to hold only 150 people, but overcrowding was common on Egyptian trains, and the jam-packed conditions were not unusual. The cost of a ticket for the 300-mile-long journey from Cairo to Luxor was less than one dollar, and people were eager to get home to celebrate a five-day festival called Eid al-Adha.

The fire started about 12:30 a.m., when the train was about forty miles south of Cairo. A passenger's small cooking stove or a gas canister used for cooking in the train's kitchen exploded, and a blaze spread quickly through the eleven train cars. The cars were so overcrowded that most people could not reach the windows. In addition, many of the tiny openings were barred, making escape impossible.

Even worse, the train's engineer did not know that a fire had broken out. The train kept moving quickly along the tracks, creating a strong breeze that fed the flames. Witnesses reported frantic passengers hurling themselves out of windows and doors to escape the burning train. Some were killed by the fall, but others survived. "I thought I was going to die anyway, so I jumped," reported one survivor. Another young man said, "I just tried to save my life. I held on until the fire made my feet and legs burn, then I let go."

The train traveled on for four miles before finally stopping. Then it took several hours for firefighters to put out the raging blaze. The flames were so hot that the train cars were burned down to their metal frames, and luggage, seats, and bodies inside had melted almost entirely.

Rescuers found hundreds of dead bodies inside the train. "The dead people were all piled up in one place in each car, like they were trying to escape," said an ambulance attendant. "It was a tunnel of death," added one survivor. At least 383 people were killed, though some speculated that the toll was higher and that the government undercounted to avoid criticism.

As the grim task of identifying bodies began, Egyptian President Hosni Mubarak quickly issued a statement expressing his sorrow regarding the disaster and calling for a complete investigation. Egypt's overcrowded trains had been involved in deadly accidents before, and security forces in the area were put on alert to handle angry families of the victims. Sadly, El Ayyat was the site of another train accident in 2009, when two trains collided and at least fifty people died.

The day after Christmas, known in many countries as Boxing Day, is usually a day of relaxation after the hustle and bustle of the holiday season. However, in 2004, a chain reaction of natural disasters made it one of the deadliest days in modern history.

Around 8:00 a.m., one hundred miles off the west coast of the island of **Sumatra, Indonesia**, an undersea **earthquake** occurred in the **Indian Ocean**. Measuring 9.1 on the Richter scale, the earthquake was the third largest ever recoded and lasted nearly ten minutes—longer than any earthquake recorded before. It caused the seabed to rise suddenly, creating a massive **tsunami**. Around fifteen minutes after the earthquake, people in the coastal Indonesian city of Banda Aceh and surrounding villages noticed that the ocean appeared to recede. Many people did not realize that this was a warning sign of the destruction to come. Just minutes later, tsunami waves up to ninety feet high crashed into the coastal city surrounding villages. Water reached nearly two miles onshore, sweeping away people, debris, and even whole buildings, transporting them up to twenty-five miles inland. Flood waters reached second and third stories of buildings, trapping and drowning thousands.

Unfortunately, that was only the beginning. Soon tsunami waves slammed the coasts of other countries in Southeast Asia and even as far away as Somalia, thirty-one hundred miles away from the epicenter. Sri Lanka and Thailand were hit two hours after Indonesia, where tourists and locals were caught off-guard by the tsunami. Whole fishing villages on India's coast were decimated. Boats and cars disappeared underwater, while resorts and hotels were flooded. A total of 227,898 people across fourteen countries lost their lives in the catastrophe, making it the deadliest tsunami event in history.

The tsunami had other devastating impacts. Over 1.7 million people were displaced as their homes were destroyed. The huge influx of saltwater and debris killed miles and miles of plants and crops, rendered farmland sterile, and destroyed freshwater sources. Hundreds of thousands of scattered bodies also made the spread of disease a huge threat in the aftermath.

The humanitarian response was swift, and nations around the world offered help to address widespread food and water shortages along with the major infrastructural damage. Donations to the affected countries totaled more than $14 billion, and the **World Food Programme** provided food aid to more than 1.3 million people.

Since the tsunami countries around the world have prioritized disaster preparedness to reduce the risk of such devastation from reoccurring. Sensors have also been installed on the ocean floor that trigger early warning signals for earthquakes and potential tsunamis in high-risk regions.

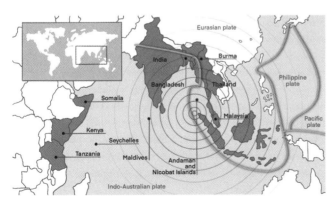

Hurricanes can be devastating, but they usually can be predicted and prepared for thanks to modern meteorology and technology. However, they can bring about unexpected complications that can prove even deadlier than the storm itself.

On Tuesday, August 25, 2005, a Category 1 hurricane made landfall near **Miami, Florida**. Many hurricanes weaken after hitting land, but **Hurricane Katrina** crossed over Florida into the warm waters of the **Gulf of Mexico**, where it quickly intensified. By Sunday, August 28, it had become one of the biggest and most powerful Atlantic storms in history, with winds spinning faster than 170 mph. The next morning, it made landfall again, but this time as a Category 4 hurricane over southeast Louisiana and Mississippi. It brought with it a **storm surge** more than twenty-six feet high in places, devastating beachfront homes and resorts along the coast. And things were about to get worse.

In the hours after Hurricane Katrina hit, it seemed that **New Orleans** had dodged a bullet. The city had avoided the most intense winds of the storm, and despite the storm surge and nearly ten inches of rainfall, New Orleans was protected from major flooding by its extensive **levee system.** However, many of the levees were old or poorly engineered, and the building water pressure soon proved to be overwhelming. Fifty-three levees across the city failed, and water came flooding in. By the end of the day on August 30, 80 percent of the city was underwater.

The mayor of New Orleans had ordered an evacuation before the storm hit, but tens of thousands of people remained in the city. As neighborhoods flooded, many people who had stayed behind had to climb on top of their roofs just to stay above the water. In some cases, they stayed there for days before they were rescued by volunteers in boats or helicopters. Hundreds were left unable to escape the flooding and were killed—some survivors recounted seeing bodies float by as they waited to be rescued.

Emergency services were unable to respond to the situation because control centers were under twenty feet of water. This led to looting and violence in many neighborhoods. Food and water shortages and rising temperatures threatened a public health catastrophe, and finally, the **National Guard** arrived on September 2 to help with evacuations along with food, water, and medical aid provisions. Soon, Canada and Mexico sent in troops, and dozens of countries donated money and supplies for cleanup and rebuilding. It was not until October 11—more than a month after Hurricane Katrina made contact—that the last of the floodwaters were pumped out.

Hurricane Katrina killed 1,836 people and became the costliest natural disaster in American history, causing more than $160 billion in damage. Several investigations concluded that the **Army Corps of Engineers**, which had designed and installed the levee system in New Orleans, was responsible for the failure. The levees were rebuilt to modern building codes, which engineers believe will help them withstand severe storms in the future.

Earthquakes have the power to cause damage wherever they strike. But unfortunately, some places are more vulnerable than others to catastrophe, and one earthquake can cause unthinkable devastation.

On January 12, 2010, at 4:53 p.m., an earthquake measuring 7.0 on the Richter scale hit fifteen miles southwest of **Port-au-Prince**, the capital of **Haiti**, and was soon followed by two strong aftershocks. The earthquakes affected Haiti and the **Dominican Republic** and could even be felt as far away as **Puerto Rico, Jamaica,** and **Cuba.** It was the biggest earthquake Haiti had experienced in more than two hundred years.

As the poorest country in the Western Hemisphere, Haiti has had a long history of subpar housing conditions, inadequate infrastructure, and nonexistent building codes. Buildings were often built on questionable foundations or wherever they would fit. The country also regularly experienced shortages of fuel, food, and water. Officials and engineers outside the country had warned for years that, for these reasons, Haiti would be especially vulnerable if faced with a major disaster. Unfortunately, these fears were correct. The earthquake left much of Haiti in ruins, severely damaging an estimated two hundred fifty thousand homes and thirty thousand commercial buildings. Even major landmarks like the **Presidential Palace**, the **Port-au-Prince Cathedral**, and the **National Assembly** building were effectively destroyed. The island's main prison was damaged, enabling many prisoners to escape, too. Thousands were killed in building collapses, especially in the heavily populated capital, while thousands more were trapped under mountains of rubble. Many hospitals were ruined, and survivors sometimes had to wait days to get medical care. Morgues were quickly overwhelmed, and corpses were stacked in the streets—some were even buried in mass graves to prevent the spread of disease.

Haiti was unprepared to handle the aftermath of the earthquake. Foreign volunteers and aid organizations rushed in, but efforts were hindered by failures with electricity, communication lines, and unreliable infrastructure. In addition, many roads in the country were blocked with debris. Even a week after the earthquake, very little food, water, and other aid had reached Port-au-Prince. Looting became more common as the meager supplies available dwindled.

On January 22, ten days after the earthquake, *Hope for Haiti Now*, aired on television stations worldwide. The charity telethon aiming to raise donations was hosted by George Clooney, Anderson Cooper, and Wyclef Jean, and featured performances by Alicia Keys, Stevie Wonder, John Legend, and Beyoncé. It became the most successful telethon of all time and raised $58 million in one day.

An estimated two hundred thousand people died in the earthquake, and many more were left homeless or displaced. The cleanup and rebuilding of Haiti would continue for more than a decade.

Deepwater drilling dozens of miles off-shore is a technique that can increase oil production and energy independence in countries around the world. However, it was also the cause of the worst environmental disaster in history.

Deepwater Horizon was a floating drilling rig located in the **Gulf of Mexico** about forty miles off the coast of Louisiana. It was chartered by oil and gas company **BP**, and on April 20, 2010, it was digging an exploratory well in more than 5,000 feet of water, attempting to locate oil that could be extracted. At 7:45 p.m., a surge of highly pressurized methane gas traveled from the well up through the tube connected to the rig. The gas blasted through several seals meant to prevent leaks like this and soon reached the rig. It ignited, causing an explosion that engulfed the platform in flames. Employees on the rig only had a few minutes to escape as the fire grew. Of the 126 people on board, 115 people were evacuated on lifeboats and by helicopter. The remaining eleven were presumed dead.

The fire on *Deepwater Horizon* continued for more than a day until the rig sank around ten o'clock in the morning on April 22. That same morning, an **oil slick** emerged around the site, and the **Coast Guard** announced that they had discovered a crude oil leak at a rate of about eight thousand barrels (equivalent to three hundred forty thousand gallons) per day. BP sent two remotely operated underwater vehicles (ROVs) down to seal the well and stop the flow of oil, but they were unsuccessful. Next, the company attempted to fit a large dome over the leak that would allow them to pump the oil out, but that failed, too. Oil would continue to flow out of the leak for eighty-seven days until it was successfully sealed with cement on September 19, 2010.

Nearly 210 million gallons of oil leaked from the well after the explosion, making it the largest marine oil spill in history. The oil affected seventy thousand square miles of ocean—about the size of the state of Oklahoma—and could be seen from space. Crews attempted to clean oil from the Gulf by skimming, siphoning, and burning it off. But this was slow, difficult work, and in May, oil began to wash up on beaches in **Louisiana**. By June, it had contaminated the beaches of **Mississippi**, **Alabama**, and **Florida,** devastating an estimated eleven hundred miles of coastline. It also killed and sickened hundreds of thousands of fish, birds, and other marine animals, and destroyed plant life in the delicate wetlands. The disaster negatively affected the Gulf Coast's tourism industry that much of the region's economy relied on.

The cleanup officially ended in April 2014, four years after *Deepwater Horizon* exploded. Investigations found that BP was ultimately responsible for the disaster and had ignored several opportunities to implement safety factors that could have prevented the spill. In April of 2016, BP agreed to pay $20.8 billion in fines for its negligence.

After the **Chernobyl disaster** (see no. 63) in 1986, many people were skeptical about the safety of **nuclear power**. However, many others felt assured that new regulations in the construction and operation of nuclear power plants would prevent future disasters. Unfortunately, twenty-five years after Chernobyl, they were proved wrong.

On March 11, 2011, just before three o'clock in the afternoon, a 9.0-magnitude earthquake occurred in the Pacific Ocean, forty-five miles east of Japan's **Oshika Peninsula**. The powerful earthquake lasted six minutes and triggered **tsunami** waves that went hurtling toward land. Less than an hour later, huge waves hit Japan's coastline, causing massive damage in the **Miyagi, Iwate,** and **Fukushima prefectures** as cities flooded and buildings washed away. The tsunami killed more than nineteen thousand people and displaced hundreds of thousands others.

Approximately fifty minutes after the earthquake, a tsunami wave over forty feet tall crashed into the **Fukushima Daiichi Nuclear Power Plant** in the town of **Okuma.** The reactors at the plant had already automatically shut off after sensing the earthquake, and because the plant had lost electricity, emergency diesel generators had automatically switched on. The electricity from these generators was needed to keep coolant circulating through the reactor's cores to prevent them from overheating. However, when the tsunami hit, the emergency generators were flooded and failed, cutting off power to the coolant pumps.

With no active cooling, three of the plant's reactors overheated, causing **meltdowns**—the radioactive material (called the fuel rod) inside the core of the reactor began to melt, burning holes in the bottoms of reactors, exposing dangerous nuclear materials, and releasing radiation. In the days after, workers furiously attempted to stop the meltdowns and provide power to the cooling systems, exposing themselves to dangerously high levels of radiation while they did so. However, a buildup of hydrogen gas from the meltdowns caused three large explosions in the buildings containing the overheating reactors, further damaging the reactors.

Because of the threat of radiation exposure, government officials ordered residents within a 19-mile radius of the facility to evacuate and established a no-fly zone for eighteen miles around the plant. More than forty-seven thousand people left their homes. By April 12, regulators announced the incident had caused a Level 7 nuclear emergency, officially elevating the Fukushima disaster to the same level as Chernobyl. It was not until eight months later that the Fukushima Daiichi plant was officially declared stable.

The disaster had severe environmental effects. Contaminated water leaked into the Pacific Ocean, sickening wildlife and endangering coastal residents. The radiation levels in the evacuation zone around the plant remained high after the disaster, making it uninhabitable.

◆ The Triangle Shirtwaist Factory Fire is considered a turning point for the improvement of working conditions around the world. However, more than a century later, workers in some countries still suffer terrible fates because of poor conditions and corporate greed.

Bangladesh is a major exporter of **textiles**, and the clothing industry has been a major factor in its economic growth since the 1970s. Many people in Bangladesh work in factories that produce textiles and garments. Several such factories were located in an eight-story commercial building called **Rana Plaza** in **Savar**, an industrial suburb of Dhaka. The building featured shops and a bank on its lower floors, and it housed five different garment factories on its upper floors. The factories manufactured clothing for brands like **Gucci, Prada, Benetton, Primark**, and **Walmart**, and employed around five thousand garment workers, most of whom were women.

On April 23, 2013, cracks appeared in the floors, pillars, and walls of Rana Plaza, and a Bangladeshi TV channel even captured footage that clearly showed this. The building was quickly evacuated. Soon, the owner of the building, **Sohel Rana**, declared that an engineer had examined the building and pronounced it safe. While the shops and bank on the lower floors remained closed until further notice, the factory workers were ordered to return the next morning. Some managers threatened to withhold up to a month's worth of pay from workers who refused to comply.

At 9:00 a.m. on April 24, the building collapsed suddenly into a pile of rubble with a deafening boom. Other workers in the neighborhood rushed to the wreckage and immediately began trying to reach survivors trapped under the debris. Search-and-rescue efforts continued for weeks after the collapse, but it was soon determined that 1,134 people died, making it the deadliest structural failure in modern history.

Investigations soon uncovered reasons that contributed to the collapse. First, Rana Plaza had a substandard foundation as it had been built on a filled-in pond. Second, it was built using poor materials, and third, the upper four floors had been added without a permit. The architect responsible claimed that the upper floors had been designed to house offices and shops, and would not have been able to properly withstand the weight and vibrations of heavy machinery. Sohel Rana was arrested four days after the collapse, charged with corruption and murder.

The collapse of Rana Plaza sparked protests and strikes by garment workers all over Bangladesh, demanding better compensation and working conditions. Advocacy groups all over the world called for **boycotts** of clothing brands linked to the factories in Rana Plaza, accusing them of exploiting cheap labor that cost hundreds of lives.

TRIVIA QUESTIONS

TEST YOUR knowledge and challenge your friends with the following questions. The answers are on the pages listed.

1. Who designed the new St. Paul's Cathedral after the Great Fire of London? (see no. 3)

2. What caused the Johnstown flood of 1889? (see no. 12)

3. What disaster encouraged the City of New York to implement fire and factory safety codes? (see no. 18)

4. What caused the *Hindenburg* disaster? (see no. 28)

5. What did residents of Florence call the volunteers who arrived to help recover and restore priceless books and works of art? (see no. 39)

6. Name three disasters that had severe impacts on the environments around them.

7. What is a limnic eruption? (see no. 64)

8. When and why were Concorde flights discontinued? (see no. 88)

9. Why did New Orleans flood so severely during Hurricane Katrina? (see no. 96)

10. What were the reasons for the Dhaka garment factory collapse? (see no. 100)

PROJECT SUGGESTION

Many of the disasters covered in this book led to changes in regulations, codes, or laws, to try to prevent similar disasters from occurring in the future. Choose one disaster and research the specific changes to rules or laws that it triggered. What exactly were these changes and why were they suggested? Is there evidence these changes have prevented a similar disaster? Can you see the impact of these rules or laws in your own life?

INDEX

OUT NOW: